Endorsements for

Delight-Full

"Truly delightful. Your heart will melt and your mouth will smile. It should be mandatory for every young mother to read this book. Kate Collins, a mother of eight young children glories in the delights of motherhood, even in the midst of sleepless nights, selfless giving, and the challenges that mothers face each day. She lives the glory of motherhood according to Psalm 113:9 where God says He makes the barren woman to be a joyful mother of children."

—Nancy Campbell, mother of 8 and editress of *Above Rubies Magazine*

"There is absolutely nothing pretentious about Kate. What you read is who she really is, and you will hear her heart and feel her love for the Lord and for her family in her words. This is experience speaking. Kate has lived it. She is speaking from real life. I have watched her over many years, and she is the real thing. I know you will be encouraged and refreshed reading *Delight-Full*."

—Beall Phillips, mother of 8 and author of *Verses of Virtue*

"Kate Collins has done all of us moms a favor in writing her sensitive and encouraging book, *Delight-Full*. I have found with my own family of fourteen children that the key to having their hearts is to make sure they know that I delight in being their mother. Children are, after all, expert heart readers, and they need to know that their sensitive hearts are in trustworthy hands. Kate has sent a challenging and uplifting wake-up call to young mothers everywhere: Number your days, realize that your children are growing up quickly, and give yourself to the precious mission of motherhood."

—Marilyn Boyer, mother of 14 and author of *For You They Signed*

"Some days it's easy to love our children. Other days, it's harder . . . when Mamma has been up for the third night in a row with a colicky baby, when the toddlers have a stomach bug, when everybody gets chicken pox . . . Some days will try a mother's patience; choosing deliberately to love their children is a choice mothers must make in obedience to God.

As a mother of seven, and now a grandmother of four little ones, I thought I had this mothering thing down, but in reading Kate's book, I learned many things that I wish I'd understood earlier. Kate Collins is one of the warmest, most loving mothers I have ever met and a wonderful example. The lives of my grandchildren (and my own!) will be richer for my having read her book."

—Mrs. Geoffrey Botkin, mother of 7 and voice of numerous audio books with the *Western Conservatory of the Arts and Sciences*

"To all mothers of young children—you are undertaking one of the most challenging yet most rewarding callings: to raise precious little ones with great love and care. The task is so great that you need encouragement for the journey from friends you can trust. Kate Collins is one of those friends. There is such sweetness, goodness, and love pouring out from the pages of her book! Her heartwarming stories and gentle advice bring back a lot of memories and priorities I had as a mommy of seven young children, and reflect a generous heart for you, young mom. You are the very one God has called to nurture the children He has given you. Let Collins and her book *Delight-Full* help you do that successfully."

—Tracy Klicka (MacKillop), homeschooling mother of 7 who blogs about marriage, family life, widowhood, and remarriage at TracyKlicka.com

"Kate Collins' book is refreshing, fun and practical, but that is only a secondary observation. Its real power took me by the hand (even as a veteran mom), gently led me beyond the obvious challenges of motherhood, and set my sight on its life-changing glory. Kate doesn't deny reality, nor does she let it taint her joy or cloud her vision of the ultimate, incredible privilege of nurturing eternal souls. She showed me how to be a better mother. Where we are tempted to fret and flounder in the daily trials of motherhood, in a culture ready to oblige us with its disdain of children, *Delight-Full* offers a timely shift back to the truth of the powerful calling on our lives. Families will be better whose moms have read this book."

—Kelly Crawford, mother of 10 and blogger at GenerationCedar.com

Delight-Full

Delight-Full

31 Days to a Happier Baby ...And Wholehearted Motherhood

Kate E Collins

VISION FORUM
Ministries®

First Printing: October 2013

Copyright © 2013 Vision Forum Ministries

8)

www.visionforum.org

ISBN 978-1-937460-69-3

Cover Design and Typography by Austin F Collins
Photography by Daniel Prislovsky

Scripture taken from the Authorized King James Version.

Printed in the United States of America

Dedication

To the One who made and whispered to my heart

To the man who holds my heart

To the sweet ones who fill my heart

. . . and my arms.

Table of Contents

Tips of the Trade

Disclaimer
What This Book Is and Is Not

What this book is not: A quick and easy "How To . . ." that will give you the happiest baby in the county in thirty-one days or less. It's not a ten-step program that will have your child reading before his third birthday. It's not even a checklist to guarantee that your baby will grow up to love you devotedly and bring you a huge bouquet of Spring's first blooms.

What this book is: A look deep into the heart of one mother at the seeds the Lord has planted there over more than a decade of raising babies. God has given us the best child-rearing manual ever written: His Word. As we apply what the Bible says to our mothering, the "whys and wherefores" of the job grow less murky, and even the third nighttime feeding in as many hours can be a moment of shared joy between Momma and Baby.

Mothering is a matter of the heart, and no amount of tips and training can substitute for the beautiful relationship that develops between mother and child when the Lord is the foundation the family is built upon *and* the mortar that holds each and every building block in place. We, as children of the Lord, look to Him for guidance, help, and love. We receive with thanksgiving these kindnesses of our Father and, in turn, pass them along to our babies. As our babies grow in stature, we grow in spiritual maturity as God fits us for the responsibility He's given to us. As we grow our children, the Lord grows us!

The contents of the chapters that follow will not deliver the result you are hoping for, Dear Reader, if you are reading this book like you would a software manual. For best results, start at the beginning, "a very good place to start." Allow the Lord to plant your heart like the lovely garden He intended it should be, and allow your family to reap the beautiful harvest that comes from His tender Hand.

Preface

A Husband's Commission

A nurturing mother is a culture changer.

Mothers who raise their babies in the nurture and admonition of the Lord are not only establishing a kingdom-building tone in their homes, but are instrumental in molding the broader culture for the advancement of the Gospel.

When I observe the world around us, I see women who are honored with the gift of motherhood and rewarded with the most precious rewards possible (Psalms 127, 128) settling for a modern-day outlook on being a mom which easily succumbs to defeat. What these mothers lack is a sense of delight in motherhood with an eye towards the grander goal of raising children who will one day shine the light of Christ in our nation and the world.

When my wife and I talked about her tackling this writing project, there were three pressing thoughts that were front and center in our minds. First and foremost, we desired to deliver the message boldly that mothers are nurturers of the next generation. The seeds they plant into the hearts of their children while they are small not only influence the youthful life of that child, but countless other lives, including that child's future spouse, children, and even grandchildren. In short, mothers help shape the culture long-term, and this is a reality that they should wholeheartedly embrace.

Generational thinking leads to the second point we wanted to make clear: Perspective is everything. Although this phrase is nearly hackneyed beyond meaning, at its core the truth is still correct. Especially in parenting. Next to loving the Lord and supporting her husband, a mother's highest calling it to pour her life into her children. And our children are only with us for a short time before they leave home to begin lives on their own: marriage, babies, jobs. When we shift our perspective to a whole-life view of our days on earth, the time we have to guide, instruct, and shepherd our children is so very short. Seeing motherhood in light of its brevity should encourage women to embrace this beautiful God-given job with their very heart of hearts.

Finally, mothers should diligently seek the tools and counsel they need as they roll up their sleeves in the most important work in their lives: raising babies for the glory of the Lord. The problem is that Grandmother is gone—the sound wisdom of generations past has been replaced with the self-centered whims of modern parenting philosophies. True wisdom hasn't been sought after for so long, many mothers do not even know where to look for it. Like buried treasure, many mothers simply don't find it because they have no map. Women may be seeking advice, but they are seeking solutions to temporal issues and not meaningful, life-changing wisdom. The greatest source of wisdom and every mother's best "treasure map," the Bible, teaches us to find answers by seeking first the "why" and then "how."

My own children are blessed by two grandmothers (and two precious great-grandmothers!) who are devoted and doting, and who love our children adoringly. But not every child is so blessed.

Young mothers today face difficult circumstances. They were raised by the hippie generation, and those hippies are today's grandmothers. Gone are the bespectacled, gray-headed, knitting matriarchs, full of life-wisdom and home remedies. Arrived are "liberated" grandmothers that e-mail their grandkids every few months and cruise the country in their RVs that are plastered with bumper stickers that read, "I'm spending my kid's inheritance!"

Today's young mothers grew up in the furnace of feminism, and though their hearts are tugging them home, they aren't sure what a God-honoring home is supposed to look like. They have questions, but are not sure where to go for answers. More often than not, there are no Titus 2 mentoring women to be found in their churches and communities. When the rarity of a true home-making grandmother is found, very often the ugly head of feminism rears within the young mother, and she balks at the biblical advice offered.

I have watched my wife struggle against the kernels of feminist thought embedded by the culture in which she was raised. And though she often describes herself as feeling like one of Cinderella's stepsisters, trying to stuff her overgrown foot into a delicate homemaking slipper, she truly glows as the love of Christ shines in her eyes, especially when she speaks of those things nearest and dearest to her heart: the Lord, her husband, and her children.

I have watched other women marvel at my wife's smile in the midst of the chaos that ensues when trying to track eight young children at the playground. I have watched grandmother-types give her kudos again and again, exclaiming they never could have done what she is doing every single day. And they all ask the same question, "How do you do it?"

I am simply amazed at how Kate loves our babies. Her heart is soft and tender, and she absolutely adores them all. She has learned much about the care of home and children, and though she is too humble to give much advice in these chance encounters, she has so much to offer. For this reason, I have commissioned her to write the following pages.

Babies cry to communicate a need, and their needs are not very complicated to understand for a mother who is tuned in to the needs of her child and knows what to look for. Yet many young mothers of today do not know what to look for.

The simplest of sound advice in raising babies, and, most importantly, the motivation—the spiritual foundation that makes up a loving mother—is a jewel that is losing ground in today's society. It's God's Word, a truth that my wife holds constantly in her heart.

Kate gathers her strength from God on the tough days and rejoices in praise to Him on the glorious days. It has only been through her dying to self, failing repeatedly and crying exhaustedly at the feet of the Lord, which has brought her to the point of seeing God bless her labors. It is through this sacrifice

that I have watched her fit beautifully into the proverbial slipper of motherhood. I've seen her struggle, cry,
and sweat. These pages are not a masterpiece of baby
schedules and child chore charts. This work is about
a mom who has learned some of the lost art of raising
babies, and who is seeing the Lord bless her efforts as
she commits them all to Him.

My wife is not yet a grandmother, and she will be
the first to tell you she is still a work in progress. But
she has earned and learned much in caring for our
eight dear children.

She is in the midst of raising our babies—twins
who just turned a year old, a three-year-old and a five-
year-old bouncing upon her knees, and four elementary
schoolers chewing on their pencil erasers, crowded
around the kitchen table for school time. The tips here
inscribed are her world, today, in real-time. I believe
that some of the lessons God has shown her can be of
great encouragement to others, most importantly, to
our own daughters.

It is primarily for our seven girls that I have asked
my precious bride to write these words as a sort of
journal. When they are grown and ask, "How did
my mom do this?" we will be able to hand this work
to our daughters with a smile, and snuggle with our
grandbabies while they sit down to read it.

While numerous other mothers inquire, we are
hopeful that, by sharing these thoughts from inside
our little world, maybe a few more homes can have
happier babies and happier mommies.

A NOTE TO HUSBANDS

Love and lead your wives. The Lord has given you the blessed responsibility to love and lead your bride. This work is only to be used as a help for those mothers with a Titus 2 relationship gap—a gaping hole, void of sound biblical mothering advice.

My wife has purposefully enveloped the following baby-raising nuggets with theological principles in order to point out the scriptural reasons behind their inclusion. You, Husband and Father, need to be aware of all that is written and discuss the principles with your wife. The Lord has made the two of you a team to raise your children together. Babies need so much from their mothers; from you, Dad, one of the most important gifts they need to receive is spiritual guidance. That job begins before your first baby is even born, as you lovingly lead your wife in the worship and love of God.

Be aware of what your wife is reading, here and elsewhere. Check claims against the truth of Scripture and pray for wisdom as together you choose the path your family will follow.

A NOTE TO WIVES

Seek your husband's counsel. This book is full of advice with a purpose, and to follow that advice will necessarily bring change to your home and family. Discuss what is found in these pages with your husband. The Lord has made you one. Seek unity as you live out the wonderful role of helpmeet to your husband and together as parents to your children.

I pray that the lessons my bride has learned will offer comfort, hope, and a view to all that God can accomplish through a mother with a willing heart and a hand, ready to be put to the plow, sowing seeds in the hearts of her children for His glory.

Austin F Collins

Introduction

From a Humble Heart

Writing has been a hobby of mine for as long as I can remember. I've spent many an hour sitting through lectures on the topic, reading style manuals and even grammar books . . . just for fun. In all of these courses and studies, one of the main "rules" of the game of writing became clear: Write what you know. In the days of yore, I thought that meant to master all available knowledge of a topic prior to writing. In those younger days, I imagined I would have to read a stack of books as tall as I am before gaining mastery of a topic in order to label myself "expert" enough to wrestle it with my pen.

Experience has taught me, though, that there are some things that thorough knowledge of all the books in the world cannot enable you to master. Reading about waterskiing, learning the techniques of the slalom and knowledge of the inboard motor that pulls you is wonderful—but words cannot begin to describe the absolutely weightless feeling of flight while gliding across the surface of the water on a misty morning just after sunrise.

Another such topic is the care and nurture of babies. Ah, babies! I _love_ babies. I always have. Ever since I was a very slim (some might say "skinny") little girl, made up entirely of knees and elbows with a lap that no baby could ever be comfortable sitting upon. I am now the mother of eight sweet, blessed babies and have plenty of fluffy padding to make them comfy snuggled up against my heart. Although I gleaned tips from books, nothing could have prepared me for the intense joys and truly heavenly love that are indelibly joined with motherhood.

As a general rule, my babies are happy, contented and truly joyful little creatures with starry eyes and long lashes that rest on their cheeks while they sleep (I can thank the Lord and my husband's beautiful-thick-hair-genes for the lashes). I had never thought much of this fact, naturally concluding that all babies are genuinely happy little critters and that the more babies you add to a family, the more the joy multiplies.

Since my twins were born (babies #7 and #8), mother after mother, grandmothers and friends have watched me, mystified as I juggled six children ten years old and younger along with their twin baby sisters. "How is it that your babies are so content?" "Your babies are so smiley!" "They are so good!" "So patient!" "So sweet!"

After being questioned again and again, I decided I would try to write a list of what exactly it is that I do to encourage my babies to be the bundles of joy they truly are. But one word answers were insufficient, and after struggling to put all that I do into simple phrases and single sentence answers, my husband summed it up beautifully.

"Doesn't it all come down to truly delighting in

your babies? That's what you do differently, Kate.
You delight in our babies every moment of every day." My
husband was spot-on. Perfect bulls-eye. But that also
raised more questions for me. Can that be the answer
I give to friends at parties and new Mommas at the
coffee shop? Does that imply that those Mommas
don't delight in their own babies? Of course not. But
there is a deeper level to true delight. Delight doesn't
form in a vacuum. It doesn't evolve from nothing. It is
created by the Author of Delight, and He has written
it upon the hearts of parents since our first parents,
Adam and Eve.

Parenting is so much more than diapers, tricycles,
and freezer cooking. Parenting is about reflecting
God to our children. Parenting is giving our children
a tangible, and very fallible, glimpse of what God's
love for them is made of.

As parents, we are to live as Christ to our children. We are to stand upon the Word of God and
teach them what unconditional love is by loving them
unconditionally. We are to teach them what self-sacrifice is by giving up the desires of our flesh to allow
these children—pieces of our own flesh—to thrive.
We are to model Christ's perfect love for His church
in our own marriages. We are to fill our homes with
the aroma of His love. The first theology lessons a
child receives begins the moment a baby is placed
in his mother's arms and he blinks his first hello to
the world. God has given us children that we might
live His gospel before them on a day-to-day, minute-to-minute basis.

We are to delight in our children because God delights in us as His children. In order for that delight to be genuine and wholehearted, we must keep our hearts in check at the Throne of Grace. These pages stem from small tips of my trade—motherhood—but they begin at the root level of my heart. Without delight in my Savior, I would not be able to bask in His delight of me, thus reflecting it to my children.

God's grace alone has made me the truly joyful mother of the eight blessings I have here on earth, and I wouldn't trade a second of even one of my busiest, craziest days (and I've included one for reference). Because of the Lord's work in my life, I can honestly say that our home is delight-full. May He bless this effort as I try to share some of the precious lessons He has taught me over the years.

In Christ Alone,
Kate

Not unto us, O LORD, not unto us,

but unto thy name give glory, for thy mercy, and

for thy truth's sake.

Psalm 115:1

1

If Home is Where the Heart is . . .

Then Feather Your Nest with Love

*And above all things have fervent charity among
yourselves: for charity shall cover the multitude of
sins. Use hospitality one to another without grudging.*
—1 Peter 4:8 & 9

Did you have a "nesting" phase at the very end of
your pregnancy? We've all heard the stories of
mothers nearing the delivery of their babies suddenly
becoming some of the most determined and dedicated
home-scrubbers in the country. For some of us, our
silver has never shone more brightly, nor our windows
sparkled so spotlessly as in the few weeks prior to the
births of our babies.

"Nesting" is a term that is met with not-so
subtle grins and sparkling eyes at my house and
among my relatives. Every time we speak of it, all
those present exchange glances, and it seems as
though they all have something dangling from the
tips of their tongues . . . though every one of them is
gracious enough not to speak it aloud. Point of fact:

I am a crazy, out-of-control nester.

My pregnancies are known throughout the land for their walloping six to nine months of hyper-emesis gravidarum. For months on end, I can't keep any sort of food or liquid down long enough to digest it. I always have to be medicated in order to stay out of the hospital due to severe dehydration. Even with the help of medication, I can only function at about half my normal level. For hours on end, as I rest on the sofa and gratefully observe my belly (and my baby!) growing, I watch dismayed as our home crumbles into messy chaos. My husband is amazing and takes over as many of my responsibilities as he possibly can, but it's been a very long time since I saw him wash the blades of a ceiling fan. Or use a feather duster to knock down the corner cobwebs. Or use a toothbrush to scrub light switches.

Just a few weeks before our twins were born, I had the sudden, uncontrollable urge to scour the exterior of our home. We lived in a century-old farm house, and the original siding had not been painted for years. I knew painting was out of the question, but scrubbing was not! I smilingly suggested it to my husband as a great Saturday activity for him and the children, but I was met with that "holding something back" expression that I often receive from loved ones when I'm in the final laps of a pregnancy.

I could see that waiting for my dear man to scrub our house would mean that I would wait longer than it would take for the babies to be born. So, like an Olympic athlete, I gave myself a great pre-game pep

talk, grabbed a push broom and scrub bucket, and
began to scour. Yes. The siding of our house. I could
reach almost to the eaves on my little step ladder.
If I stretched. And extended the long handle of the
broom. But even in my nesting-induced thought-fog,
I knew better than to climb a full size ladder carrying eleven pounds of babies and their accompanying
placentas, etc. in my ever increasing girth.

Three sides of the house were scrubbed to my satisfaction, and rinsed with the hose before my strength
gave out. I was utterly exhausted, but I felt great about
my clean house. I sat in a rocking chair on the front
porch, slowly rocking the babies in my belly with a
huge smile of serenity on my face.

Looking back, I can clearly see the absolute ri-
diculousness of my nesting urges. But at the moment,
they seem so real and needful. And truly, we *should* be
preparing our homes for our babies. But that preparation begins within our hearts as mothers. Our welcoming attitudes and our warm, welcoming arms are
much more valuable to a baby than manicured lawns
or scrubbed baseboards.

Opening her home—and her heart—to a baby
means that a mother is prepared to give of herself in
order to make her baby comfortable. She will be willing to give up sleep with a smile to better care for her
baby. She will gladly watch her own dinner grow cold
so that her baby can be fed when he is hungry. She
will give every ounce of her strength, and then a little
more, in order to see her baby tucked snugly into bed
after an all-night visit to the emergency room for an

over-the-top high fever.

Giving generously does not mean that we give without thought because it's "only the best" for our babies. Does a baby need designer clothes from elite boutiques to be happy and contented? Does he expect a sprig of parsley to garnish his highchair tray while he eats his toasted oat cereal? Should we really be willing to spend whatever it takes to make sure that our babies are enrolled in Mommy-and-Me swimming classes at six months of age? Giving from the heart is so much more valuable than giving from the wallet alone.

As in practicing hospitality with any person, that which we give is only as precious as the heart that delivers it. A brand new SUV with side airbags will not drive a baby home from the hospital perceptibly smoother than a trustworthy decade-old vehicle. The most expensive cradle in the catalog will not help a baby to sleep any better than he might in the hand-me-down crib from his cousin. A cold and sterile home filled with baby gear covered by all the bells and whistles cannot make a baby feel at ease. A salaried nanny cannot possibly offer the unconditional love a baby craves from his mother.

As mothers, we need to be less concerned with the age and state of our furniture and flooring, and more concerned with the love that permeates every corner of our homes. We want our families, and those who visit our homes, to feel kick-off-your-shoes cozy when they step across the threshold. We need to create a space where our family *wants* to be.

The Lord has blessed mothers with the capabilities for nesting. As we feather the nest that He has provided for us, we need to be grateful for what we have and ready to give it all back to Him in service to those in need. And He has given those with the most need and utter dependency right into our laps, in the forms of a precious babies.

As we welcome the cherished little ones that God sends to our families, we need to remember that our goal as Christian mothers is to point their footsteps to their Creator. And in raising children in a home that welcomes all by its love that comes from Him alone, we can help them to begin that journey from their very first days.

Love (Your Baby) *Notes*

Welcome your baby into your home with open arms. He or she is a part of the family—not just an observer or simply an object to be moved around. Include your baby in the moment-to-moment action of the home!

2

Your Baby is a Priceless Treasure

Savor Everything about Your Baby

Ye are bought with a price. . . . —1 Corinthians 7:23

O ne of our family's favorite traditions takes place on the anniversary of my husband's and my wedding day. We usually dine on a lovely meal at home that evening and bring out photos of a very young Momma and Daddy, all dressed up for their wedding day. Then, after stories and remembrances and a yummy dessert, we dig my bridal gown out of its storage place.

After our marriage, my thoughtful mother had my dress cleaned and vacuum-sealed, to preserve its color and pristine beauty. It was returned from the dry cleaners in a stout cardboard box with a plastic "peek-a-boo" window over the top, so whenever I wanted to look at it, I could simply peek under the lift-the-flap lid, much like our children's board books. When our three eldest daughters were three years, nearly two years, and four months old, I dusted off the box and placed it on the floor to allow our girls to peek under the flap.

I beamed and the children oohed and ahhed and clamored to get a better view through the plastic covering. In all the commotion, one of the girls rested her little palms upon the plastic "window," and pressing down, broke the vacuum-pack seal. I gasped, and my daughters froze, gaping with wide eyes at me.

"Oh!" I said, trying to keep the upbeat and cheerful atmosphere alive and failing miserably. "It's okay. But let's put away the dress now."

My sweet little girls did not complain, and the evening moved on towards bedtime, but the knot in my stomach over my bridal dress and its exposure to the air only tightened as the evening went on. We had invested money in this gown, and countless memories were attached to it. I was truly troubled about a heap of satin, beading, and pouf!

As He always is, the Lord was gracious with me and my silly propensity to cling to the "treasures" of this world. He opened the eyes of my heart to see the dress for what it truly is: a pile of satin, beading, and pouf. Worth very little, and only valuable because of what it represented: the first day of the writing of our family's history.

When our anniversary rolled around again the following year, my little girls remembered what had happened to the keepsake box, and were very, very careful not to touch it. When I broke open all the seals with reckless abandon, they gaped at me again, this time with even wider eyes than the previous year.

"This year, girls, you get to try Mommy's dress

on!" The smiles that radiated from their faces rivaled mine the first time I wore the dress. Those sweet grins on those precious faces were far more valuable than the paltry dress I had been so worried to preserve.

Every year, my girls and I twist their hair up into fancy "up-dos" and pin my veil on the top. Then the real fun begins: they climb into Momma's gown. When they are very little, their tiny faces are engulfed by all that pouf! But we now have a series of photos of each sweet daughter, growing year after year, as she tries on my dress. We have a

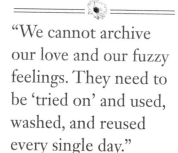

"We cannot archive our love and our fuzzy feelings. They need to be 'tried on' and used, washed, and reused every single day."

beautiful "measuring stick" in photos of their growth, and a visible reminder that our time with them is so very short. Out of a small accident grew a priceless and precious yearly tradition that I wouldn't trade for all the pouf in North America!

Every sweet dimple, every tiny toe, and every sparkling grin of our children is growing—every moment of every day. I need to remind myself as a mother, that, in caring for all the needs of these sweet little people, I must not forget to soak in the goodness of these fleeting days. While I try to preserve the "packaging" of our family—some semblance of order in the home, school work supervised and complete, meals cooked, kitchen cleaned, laundry washed and ironed—my real treasures, my children—need to be loved, cuddled, and adored. We cannot archive our love and our fuzzy feelings. They need to be "tried on" and used, washed, and reused every single day.

Even as we treasure our children, the Lord cherishes us—His children—even more. He purchased us from the slavery of our sin with the blood of his very own Son. We are bought at a price (1 Corinthians 7:23). The love He has for us is simply unfathomable.

And yet, we are to live out an example of this love to our babies daily. And although we will fail, and often, we can come to the Lord in repentance, asking Him for the strength to love our children as we ought. We need to tear the proverbial plastic wrapping off of our hearts with reckless abandon, so that we don't simply archive our warm fuzzy emotions.

Our children need to see us cherish them for the priceless gift that they are. Although we do need to care for the needs of our children, both physical and spiritual, they need to know they are loved above all else. Not because a daughter looks beautiful in a starched white blouse. Not because a son is being helpful by unloading the dishwasher. But because they are the children that God has entrusted to us.

Every person has the need to be loved. When the Lord has whispered to the heart of a person, and she knows she is loved by God, that need is met forever and ever, amen! But until each of our children understand that unconditional, unending Love, Mommas offer them a pale, earthly example.

Our love for our children needs to reflect God's heart. And someday, by His grace alone, we will see their own hearts brimful to overflowing with Love from the very Source Himself.

Love (Your Baby) *Notes*

Savor every sweet dimple, every tiny toe, every sparkling grin. Treasure the gift of motherhood for the gift it truly is.

3

Fill Your Home with Music

Sing a Song in Your Heart

O sing to the Lord a new song: sing unto the Lord, all the earth. Sing unto the Lord, bless his name; shew forth his salvation from day to day. —Psalm 96:1 & 2

My husband, Austin, is very gifted in so many areas of life. In fact, when we were just beginning to know each other, my mother described him as "multi-faceted." And the longer I know and love him, the more I agree with that assessment! He is strong and athletic. He is a very creative artist and designer. He is not afraid to tackle building projects, or electrical or plumbing repairs. He climbs mountains. He kayaks rivers. He makes up amazing pterodactyl stories on the spot. And his scrambled eggs are the best I've ever eaten.

One of his gifts that especially blesses our family is his gift of music. He plays acoustic and bass guitar and loves to make up songs . . . about everything from putting on shoes to brushing teeth to loading up in the car. Just last night, as we sat down for dinner, he announced that it was a "sing everything you need to say" meal. What a hoot! Our children have a great appreciation for music in all its forms, because it's such a key part of our life together.

Austin is most comfortable playing his acoustic guitar, and our children are captivated by his music when he does so. Especially our babies. I have photographs of all of our children, as crawling babies, climbing into his lap and inspecting his guitar and its strings, feeling its sound through the polished wood. The older children laugh and exclaim as the baby grabs the fretboard and makes discordant sounds and squeaky scratches, and that encourages the baby even more.

My husband is a wonderful balance of sheer manhood and artistic ability; a blend of toughness and tenderness. He is very much how I envision King David of the Bible. His heart is absolutely devoted to the Lord, and he delights in expressing that devotion through song. I am so grateful to be a witness to his sharing his love of the Lord with our babies as he worships through music! Music is expressive of every human emotion. Without laborious explanations and definitions, our children can know by the tones, pace, and key what emotion is being expressed through the notes of a song.

Did you ever wonder what notes King David wrote to accompany his poetical psalms? So many of the Psalms are introduced by the phrase, "To the chief Musician, A Psalm of David." David chose music and poetry to beautifully describe his joy and triumph, his despair and desolation, his victory and defeat. The Psalms are a record of a man's life—a man after God's own heart—and it is all written to music (Acts 13:22).

Have you ever noticed that babies stop crying almost instantly when you sing to them? Our twins are in the stage where they try to wiggle when it's time for a diaper change. Time and training are required for every baby to learn that the changing table is not the place for "chase me" as they try to squirm away. When they begin to fuss about holding still, I begin to sing what is happening. My voice is not great, and my pitch is not perfect, but all of our babies have loved this. Their eyes lock onto mine and huge, toothless grins illuminate their faces . . . and they hold still to hear the melodious notes about wipey-dipes and powder, fresh diapers and cream. Insert a few kisses on tiny toes or a zerbert on the belly, and this song could easily make the Baby's Top Ten list of greatest hits. Will these little dittys make their way to an album for children some day? Not a chance. Will my little ones remember the words? Not likely. But they will remember a smiling Momma, even in the midst of the worst of messes, rather than a Grumpy Baby vs. Grumbling Momma wrestling match.

As Mommas who wish to introduce our babies to the truths of the Lord, shouldn't we strive to fill our homes with the loveliest aspects of that truth? One of the simplest ways to do so is through the melodies and harmonies that breathe glory to the Creator of all things lovely. Music can so easily ensnare and entangle the emotions, but when we train our babies from their earliest days to recognize music for what it truly is—a vehicle to bring glory to the Lord— they can grow up in the footsteps of King David, pouring out their very souls to God in the heart of a melody.

Music is a bit like playing with matches. Used properly, it can light a flame of passion for the Lord that is inextinguishable. Used improperly, music can ignite a wildfire of passions for the fleshly things of this world. As parents, we must pray for wisdom and discernment as we introduce our children to music.

Imagine what the Lord could do with a generation of babies raised to give Him glory through song! When we devote our time and our talents to God, with His blessing, we are one step closer to truly understanding what it means to love Him and enjoy Him . . . forever.

Love (Your Baby) *Notes*

Introduce your baby to different types of music, and how each type sets the tone for the home: orchestral classics for reading and sleep, fiddle tunes for dancing, brass for marching, etc., then join your baby in the action!

4

Heart to Heart

Talk with Your Baby

*A good man out of the good treasure of his heart
bringeth forth good . . . for of the abundance of the
heart his mouth speaketh. —Luke 6:45*

When I was a young baby, just learning to crawl
fast enough to make grown-up types take notice of all the choke-ables I was eager to consume, my
grandparents came for a visit. I'm sure they oohed and
aahed over me, as all loving grandparents are wont to
do, and then settled in for a nice, long catch-up chat
with my father and mother.

In the midst of this conversation, a big, slow-mov-
ing, aptly-named bumble bee landed on the yellow
and orange shag carpet a few yards from where I was
busy exploring the big new world of the living room.
Full of curiosity, I crawled towards the bumble bee as
fast as my chubby hands and knees could carry me.
My grandfather saw what I was after, and jumped up
to step on the bee. Although he did, in fact, squish the
insect, it was somewhat cushioned by all that lovely,
soft carpet. Rather than pick up the seemingly dead
bug, my grandpa went back to his conversation with

19

my parents. I promptly snatched up the bee in my plump palm and tried to stick it in my mouth.

The bee had just enough life left in it to sting me directly on my bottom lip. As the story goes, I absolutely howled! And my lip blew up to three times its normal size. My poor grandfather felt so terrible, he was nearly ill.

In Proverbs chapter 16, verse 24, we read that "Pleasant words are as an honeycomb, sweet to the soul and health to the bones." I've never met a person who did not like honey. Our children would add honey to everything they eat if we would allow it. Our favorite Saturday morning treat of pancakes usually swim in a pool of honey upon the plates of our children. Sweet goodness for their tummies as well as their hearts!

Ironically, one of the sweetest treats the Lord provides in His creation is created by one of the hardest-working and surprisingly sharp-ended creatures: the honey bee. One would never guess that this small insect that has the ability to make such a delicious treat could pack such a nasty punch in its stinger. Yet, that stinger is always hiding, ready to zing the person who becomes troublesome.

How often do our children expect sweetness from us, their Mommas, only to be stung by angry words and a sour attitude? It is with too much ease that we become like the bee: soft on the outside, maybe even filling our day with sweet good works, but delivering a sting with our untamed and unguarded tongues when we are annoyed.

James writes, "But the tongue can no man tame; it is an unruly evil, full of deadly poison" (James 3:8). My tongue is so apt to lead me into trouble! There are times I literally have to rest my chin on my hand while listening to another in order to keep my mouth closed and "hold my tongue." So often, I have neglected to rein in my galloping words and have uttered hurtful or resentful words that I can never round up, nor repair the damage they have inflicted.

Our words as mothers are a tool that we can use to build up our families or squelch the beauty that could be so abundant in the home. Either way, we teach our children through our actions and *the words we speak.* The contents of our words are an audible lesson preached daily to the ears of our little ones, and if left unguarded, our tongues can leave the stinging traces of venom. How much more we should long to leave honey in the memories of our babies!

"The contents of our words are an audible lesson preached daily to the ears of our little ones, and if left unguarded, our tongues can leave the stinging traces of venom."

The contents of our hearts is made manifest in our words (Luke 6:45), and this includes tone, facial expressions, and volume. Babies respond with utmost trust to the nurturing of their mothers. Our hearts need to be filled with the Word of God in order to offer truth to our children. Our hearts need to be grateful to the Lord so we can sing songs of thanksgiving with our children. Our hearts need to be humble so that we are teachable and better able to teach our children.

I have no memory of the bumble bee incident described above, but it was told and retold to me throughout my growing up years. And in that, I have discovered another sweet blessing of God: forgetfulness. The highlights and headlines are what stand out in memory. Just as mothers often forget the sheer difficulty and pain of giving birth, remembering only the joy of holding a newborn, so our children—when raised in loving, God-desiring homes—tend to remember the good times of their young years. With the Lord's help and a firm hand of self-control on the leash that holds our tongues, we can fill up their days with sweet goodness . . . so our children's cup of memories will be filled to the brim with lovely memories to recall and recount to their own children in future years. We need to repent of past failures, and pour honey in to the hearts—and ears!—of our babies. Today! And every day hereafter.

Love (Your Baby) *Notes*

Talk to your baby—not baby talk, but animated conversation. You'll notice that it won't be a one-sided chat. Your baby will respond with sweet faces, smiles, and coos!

5

S.O.S.

When Your Baby Speaks His Mind

My sheep hear my voice, and I know them, and they follow me. . . . —John 10:27

Every few years, our family has a knock-down, drag-out fight with illness. And it continues all winter long. Weeks at a time of coughing, runny noses, sore throats. For months on end. As soon as we recover from one virus, another sneaks into the house, and the vicious cycle starts all over again. This year, we had so many sick days, I was always "waiting for the other shoe to drop" so to speak when everyone seemed healthy for more than a few days at a time, fully expecting that our next bout with sickness was just around the corner.

Although exhausting physically and emotionally, all these sick weeks allowed us much more time to snuggle and cuddle, tucked into warm quilts. And we were able to read several wonderful books aloud as we rested and convalesced. Until I became sick with the same horrible virus that had been affecting our twins for a week or so. My lungs filled with gunk, and my nose ran, and my voice became a raspy, scratchy, weak-as-see-through-coffee version of its former self.

Losing one's voice is a nuisance at best, and truly dangerous at worst. I could not call the children to lunch when it was piping hot and ready. My voice failed me when our two-year-old was running her fastest, and I was trying to cheer her on. Only a squeak escaped my throat when the babies crawled with alacrity to climb the stairs when the baby gate was mistakenly left open. I was left with no choice but to jump and run after a child on several occasions because I simply could not make my voice work to issue a warning or ask for help. Mothering became incredibly hard to navigate when I had no voice to call out to my children to offer advice or direction.

Verbal communication is a vital part to every relationship. Think of all the topics of conversation that must be covered between you and your husband: scheduling, budgeting, child rearing, and soul-deep spiritual truths. And each of these items is then translated into child-speak through on-time pickups, grocery store choices, a united child-training front, and Bible teaching throughout every day. Every solid relationship is built upon not only speaking one to another, but truly hearing what is being communicated.

Imagine if you and your husband chatted one evening about adjusting your budget and decided together that you would switch to using cloth diapers in order to save in the grocery budget. Imagine what he would say when you wobbled through the door the following afternoon with three warehouse-sized boxes of disposable diapers stacked under your chin!

Obviously, the communication lines became crossed somewhere in this scenario.

It's very much the same for a baby whose only "voice" for communicating is through crying. Imagine a baby who is crying to let his mother know that his diaper needs a change, and she thrusts a bottle of apple juice into his mouth instead of offering clean pants. Or think of a baby who wakes up for a new day and issues a "Good morning! Let's play!" sort of cry . . . and her mother swoops in and scoops her up, very tenderly "soothing" what she perceives is her sad and upset baby. Sounds ridiculous, doesn't it?

Oftentimes, as Mommas, we become so wrapped up in our adult cares and grown-up thoughts, that we forget to take the time to really hear what our babies are trying to say through their crying. The cries of an infant are definitely not all the same, and once you become a student of them, it is much easier to decipher just what that wee person is trying to "say." We need to learn to hold off for half a second when we hear crying, and truly try to understand just what a baby might be asking for. Each and every cry is not an S.O.S. signal, and mothers need to remember that crying should not equate to stress-induced responses from us.

Part of learning what your baby is saying is to study the patterns of his day. Does he usually become sleepy at about 10 a.m. for a morning nap? Then his fussing at 9:50 should let you know that he's ready to sleep a bit early after his morning's excitement. Does your baby always cry at about 5:30 p.m. when you are preparing dinner for the rest of the family? Perhaps Baby needs a snack to tide him over until the family eats together at 6:45. Does your baby become overwhelmed when too many people hold him in a short period of time? Then his upset outburst with Aunt Mildred is truly just his way of saying that he needs a break from the crowd. Getting to know your baby allows you to guess with much accuracy what message his crying at a specific moment is meant to say.

When I lost my voice, I found it so distressing when trying to communicate with my children. Oftentimes, they could not understand my meaning, and I would simply sigh and give up trying to explain. How thankful I am that the Lord Jesus never shrugs and walks away from me! He tells us in John that His sheep know His voice, and they follow Him. Not only do the sheep *hear*, but they *do*. When we have His Word hidden in our hearts, and His Word on our tongues, we are able to walk the path He has set before us, and lead our children the same way.

We need to be good listeners so that our faith will be lived forth in accordance with His plan for us. Our Momma-hearts need to be based on Scripture, and our actions will follow (James 2:20). We *teach* our children to listen well, when we *show* them how to listen well.

Conversation, and likewise relationship, is a two-direction avenue. Only talking benefits no one— it's akin to playing tennis against a wall. The person holding the racket cannot improve in skill because she is only returning her own serve. In order to have a relationship that delves deep in the hearts of two individuals, one must be prepared to offer and receive. "Iron sharpeneth iron; so a man sharpeneth the countenance of his friend" (Proverbs 27:17). Oftentimes, Mommas do all the "serving" with their babies, never allowing their babies to truly communicate with them.

As Mommas, we have been granted the gift of teaching a tiny person how to relate! We can teach them how to speak and respond, how to offer information, how to converse. But we must also teach them to listen well and to hear the hearts of those to whom they speak. Because all that we teach them in our homes is only practice for when they are grown and living their faith on their own. They must know how to hear their Creator's voice and respond fully to Him. What a gift! And what a responsibility!

May He open the ears of our Momma-hearts so we might be fully ready to respond to His tender voice in living out our faith daily before our families. And may He make us each a sweet example for the little ones at our feet who are learning daily from what they see when they look up to us.

Love (Your Baby) *Notes*

Observe your baby, learn to know his or her responses, and respond to his or her cues. Don't pounce on every noise, assuming it's an S.O.S. Crying is a baby's communication tool.

6

The Eye of the Storm

Fill Your Heart with Peace

I will not leave you comfortless: I will come to you . . .
Peace I leave with you, my peace I give unto you: Not
as the world giveth, give I unto you. Let not your
heart be troubled, neither let it be afraid.
—John 14:18 & 27

In the final months of 2012, Hurricane Sandy swept north along the eastern seaboard of the United States and left a wide wake of devastation behind it. Businesses were boarded up, and coastal homes destroyed. In some areas, electricity and telephone service were off for months following the storm. Lawlessness filled the streets and repairmen were accosted by truly desperate residents. Families were uprooted, like so many trees, and left to try to pick up the pieces as best they could with the meagre resources available. The devastation crossed state and cultural lines and created turmoil where once busy and productive citizens carried out their daily tasks.

We have all seen satellite photos of hurricanes: the huge white swirl that looks like an enormous and vicious version of the foam that covers a latte, only it covers a third of the Atlantic Ocean. There are four main parts to every hurricane: the eye, the eye wall, rain bands, and rain shields.

The eye is a relatively calm area, with lighter winds and hardly any precipitation. In fact, there are reports that sometimes as the eye passes over land, people on the ground have seen blue sky or stars, depending on the time of day! The eye wall is where the fiercest and most violent parts of the storm swirl around the eye. Raging thunderstorms and heavy rains pulse around the center and often bring the most destruction. The rain bands surround the eye wall and spiral out from the center, carrying large amounts of rain and high winds with each band. Interestingly, the rain bands contain much of the evaporation and condensation that fuel the hurricane. Finally, rain shields are the name given to the points of the hurricane where the deluge truly happens. These solid areas of rain become even more full of precipitation the nearer to the eye they are found.

It is easy to imagine family life as a hurricane. The eye wall represents the members of the family—trying to fit so many lives into one house, along with all their activities and personalities. It can feel at times like several thunderstorms all raging at once! The rain bands are our interactions with the world: neighbors, church, library, sports practice, music lessons, grocery store, etc. There are many people outside the family that hold sway over our children. The rain shields are simply the busyness that threatens to consume our time and drown our domestic harmony.

The rain comes in the form of text messages, e-mails, media in several forms, work schedules, needs of friends . . . Life can be overwhelmingly busy and full of chaos if we allow it to be so.

Consider for a moment what it must feel like to be at the absolute center of a hurricane. I remember forecasters warning those residents who chose not to flee the path of the oncoming storm to be aware of the "calm" in the midst of the storm. The warnings were generally all the same: "Do not go outside! It is only the eye of the storm, and the fierce winds will begin again shortly. Do not be fooled into thinking the storm is over! Keep under cover!"

As mothers, *we are the eye in the center of the hurricane* that swirls around our families and our homes. There are so many trite analogies to describe the world: a howling wilderness, a vast wasteland, a dog-eat-dog free-for-all. Our children need to know that when they come home—to Momma—they will be met with a smile and a warm hug. They *do not* need to be met by Mother in heels and pearls serving fresh cookies. What matters most to every little person is the calm heart that beats in the center of that welcoming hug in the midst of life's storm.

One of my dearest friends has a houseful of boys—seven to be exact, and two daughters. She is

> "What matters most to every little person is the calm heart that beats in the center of that welcoming hug in the midst of life's storm."

the perfect embodiment of peace in the center of swirling chaos. Her boys check in on her throughout their adventures: one showing her the praying mantis he caught; another giving her a drawing of a pirate; the next asking her if he might build a new tree house with Daddy's power tools?; the list goes on endlessly. I learned one of my most valuable mothering lessons from this friend: a peaceful heart is a decision. Being flustered by our surroundings happens by default. Giving our families the gift of peace and calm in the center of the storm of life is a minute-by-minute, prayer-filled determination that the Lord blesses with the gift of familial harmony.

We need to live our lives in the Peace that Passes Understanding—offering a respite for our babies and our older children from the storm-tossed world outside our front door. We need to work our hardest to make sure that our children do not become the "eye wall," each trying to outdo each other to be the loudest, most demanding and most controlling person in the home. We need to model peace, understanding, and a servant's heart. When we teach our children to serve others—and each other!—life is made smoother for all members of the family.

"… a peaceful heart is a decision. Being flustered by our surroundings happens by default."

Mothers need to provide the place where our children can look up in the center of a storm and see the blue sky. We need to teach them to look up and see the stars! And to see the Creator of the stars, Who wants so much more for their lives than busyness and chaos. The Lord does not leave us comfortless. He has provided His Word and the Holy Spirit to guide us every step of the way. It is our job as mothers to point our children to this Guide who whispers to their hearts.

Momma needs to *be* calm, to *orchestrate* a calm spot in the lives of her children so they might truly hear His beautiful whisper.

Love (Your Baby) *Notes*

Fill your heart with peace. This can only be accomplished by keeping the eyes of your heart focused on the Prince of Peace at every moment.

7

Uniquely You

Be the Best Momma
That God Made *You* to Be

*I will praise thee; for I am fearfully and wonderfully
made: marvellous are thy works; and that my soul
knoweth right well. —Psalm 139:14*

About two weeks after the birth of our sixth baby,
a dear friend and mentor called to see if she
could stop by the following day for a quick visit and
to deliver something delicious for dinner. My mother
was staying with our family to help me along in my
recovery by caring for our other five children, who
were eight years old and younger. I was thrilled that
the two of them could finally meet! I enthusiastically
agreed and made sure the house was picked up a bit
before I went to bed.

That night was a low-sleep night, as the baby was
up frequently. My mom had heard her crying, and
graciously allowed me to sleep a bit later than usual in
the morning. She had seated the children around the
breakfast table when I was startled out of my sleep by
her clearly agitated voice. It took me a few moments

to truly comprehend what she was saying:

"There is a skunk in the mudroom! Quick!"

I leapt out of bed and ran barefooted to the windows that offered a view of the mudroom, and my heart sank at the sight. There was our big, happy-go-lucky lab munching away on her kibble, blissfully unaware of the drama that was unfolding. A tiny, juvenile skunk had meandered into the mudroom, probably drawn by the aroma of dog food. About two seconds after I arrived at the scene, and before I could utter a word, the dog turned and met the skunk eyeball to eyeball. Both were startled by the sight of the other, and our dog jumped back. The skunk jumped and . . . you guessed it, let loose with his unmistakable and almost unbearable spray. Inside our mudroom. He skittered away, through the open screen door and I stood, eyes wide and mouth gaping.

My mother and I gagged, overwhelmed by the odor, and the children began talking excitedly and all at once. My mind raced as to the best course of action, but my thoughts swam in the stink and nothing seemed to make sense. Finally, I figured I should just march boldly into the mess. Still in my pajamas, I donned yellow plastic gloves, grabbed a bottle of hydrogen peroxide, a bottle of dish soap and the box of baking soda, and conducted my scientific, chemical-reaction de-skunking process.

"If you could just get some breakfast into the kids, and help them get dressed. Remember Dorys is coming at ten?" I called over my shoulder to my mom as I carried my bubbling brew outside.

It was a race against the clock. I tied the dog to a fence post and poured my neutralizing concoction over her fur. I began to scrub. And scrub. And scrub. Our dog is ninety pounds and not fond of baths under the best of circumstances. My mind began to wander into the territory of self-pity.

"I just had a baby! I *do not* need to be scrubbing this silly dog! *Other* mothers get to stay in bed for weeks after giving birth, and here I am, wrestling with this huge, stinking dog!" The dog's ears drooped lower and her tail was between her legs. Her fur was foamy all over. I had mud splashed up to my knees and smudges and bubbles all over my face. My hair was in a loose ponytail that was hanging in my eyes. I was a disheveled mess, inside and out. Just then I heard my mom calling to me from inside the house. I wondered what she could need me for, but there was the call again.

I clomped my muddy shoes through the smelly mudroom and poked my head in the door. The newborn was crying and the other children were again speaking over one another in a cacophony of voices.

"We have another small crisis," explained my mother. "The kids were playing trains and, well, one didn't make it to the bathroom in time."

"Can you just use a work towel to sop it up?" I asked, a bit exasperated.

"It wasn't that sort of accident," answered my dear mom. Realization broke upon me and I was thankful I had my rubber gloves already on. My mom tried to comfort the baby since I was covered in wet dog and skunk. We drew a bath for said child, and I got out the bleach spray and cleaned up the trail left across the house. I heaved a sigh and tromped back through the oily-odor laden mudroom. I began feeling sorry for myself again.

"Why do I always end up in the middle of these ridiculous situations? No one else I know faces days like this!" I thought as I moped across the yard to my drooping dog.

When I reached her, I noticed that the smell wasn't strong around her. There was hardly any trace of skunk. I stuck my nose close to her fur—near her face, neck, back, rump. There was no skunk smell on the dog. And it wasn't due to my amazing deskunking mix. The dog hadn't been sprayed in the first place. The little skunk had been so startled that it didn't know which way to turn or run, and his aim was off. His odiferous residue was plastered against the mud-room door.

I sighed again and rinsed the dog, then toweled her off. And I trudged inside to take a shower, hoping to clean up my attitude along with my muddy self, thinking again how nice it must be to have the sort of life where new Mommas are spared some of the nastiest duties of daily life. But truly, does anyone live that sort of life?

Mommas tend to imagine that our friends live in sparkling homes with clean carpets and dusted furniture. We imagine their children with spot-free clothes and shining faces, neatly completing their work assignments for school. We imagine their husbands bringing them flowers at the end of a tough day, and maybe even a takeout pizza so cooking dinner isn't necessary. The key word here is *imagine*. This sort of world exists only in imagination.

In real life, we all face trials great and small.

Mommas often trip headlong into the pit that is comparison. We measure our bodies, our children, our husbands, our houses, our curriculums and everything else against those we see around us. Comparison accomplishes nothing but breeding self-pity and discontent (2 Corinthians 10:12). The Bible tells us to be content in all our circumstances (Philippians 4:11). Why? Because the Lord handpicks our circumstances for us. He allows only those trials which will enable us to better turn our faces to Him. He allows the trials that will best prune away the unsightly growths on our hearts so that they better reflect His image.

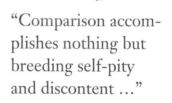

"Comparison accomplishes nothing but breeding self-pity and discontent ..."

Proverbs 31:25 tells us that the godly woman "will rejoice in the time to come." She looks ahead and knows that trials and snares are in her path but she rejoices in the knowledge that the Lord will keep her steady and safe. Many times in my own life, I've read about the Proverbs 31 woman and sighed inwardly. Her accomplishments, her attitudes, her helpfulness seem so unattainable. But this chapter is a snapshot of her life. It is the highlights of what we should aim for as

41

Christian women. She offers a great example of *choosing* to rejoice.

Oftentimes, we cannot change the circumstances of our lives. But we can change our responses to them. There are many days when everything seems to go wrong, and I force myself to acknowledge that I can either laugh or cry. The best option for my children is when I choose to laugh.

The Lord allows skunks to wander into our lives at times. But I cannot allow myself to assume that I am the only woman in the world to have to face down a skunk with all his residual stench.

My sweet friend did come by to visit that skunky day, and brought along her new daughter-in-law that I had previously met just a few times. My mom and I did all we could to clean up the messes and disguise the skunk smell by lighting every candle I owned before they arrived. As I sat on the sofa, trying to relax and enjoy the company, I realized that I could pretend like nothing had happened that morning and that we just really liked candles. Or I could make the choice to laugh and give my friends the chance to laugh along with me. And we did. Heartily! They cooed over the baby as they snuggled with her, and we shared a lovely morning together.

As Christian mothers, we need to stop comparing ourselves to others, and focus more on encouraging each other in the Lord. You may have a friend who loves to be creative and makes her own birthday cards. You may have a friend with a high mess tolerance who allows her children to make their own salt dough and then build their creations on the kitchen floor. You may have a friend who keeps her house as clean and sparkly as a museum. None of that matters if you are seeking to encourage her by speaking about that which really matters: the works of God in her life and in the lives of those she loves (Proverbs 31:26).

God made *you*, just as you are. He chose *you* to be the mother to your children. He chose *you* to be the wife to your husband. He chose *you* to be the daughter to your parents and the sister to your siblings. These are the only jobs you will ever hold in which you are irreplaceable. Choose do to these jobs well. Choose to be thankful for the gifts that the Lord has given to you and try to grow in the areas that have rough edges. Choose to rejoice in the days to come, because you will be facing them hand-in-hand with the One who created them—and you!—and spoke them into being.

Love (Your Baby) *Notes*

Comparisons crush the spirit. Comparing yourself to another mother crushes the zest out ssof life. Be the Momma that God created you to be and do your best at it.

8

Uniquely Your Baby

Your Baby is One of a Kind Too

> *. . . thou has covered me in my mother's womb. I will praise thee; for I am fearfully and wonderfully made: marvellous are thy works; and that my soul knoweth right well.* —Psalm 139:13 & 14

> *Keep thy heart with all diligence; for out of it are the issues of life.* —Proverbs 4:23

Our second-born is known for her pure and utter sweetness. She has a face that is almost continuously wreathed in smiles. She cares for her younger siblings with joy and delight and sings praises to the Lord throughout the house—our own little songbird! This tender-hearted darling has always been such.

When she was about two years old, we had a grapefruit-sized plush stuffed bear that had a gel-filled middle. It lived in the freezer; it was the ideal companion when one of our little ones had a bumped head or scraped knee. What a fantastic invention! Not only were our children soothed by the cool compress, but they had a moment to cuddle with a sweet bear that was hidden away and pulled out only for "owie" moments.

One day, our sweet little girl broke the house rules in some small way. I looked at her with my eyebrows scrunched together, and my mouth held in a firm frown.

"Oh no! We don't do that—no, no!" I scolded. Her sweet, tender heart melted into a puddle of weepy tears, and she called out for "the bear" through her trembling lips and quivering chin.

Confused, I looked at her in wonder, but retrieved the sought-for bear from the freezer. My sweet, loving and gentle little girl grasped that fuzzy blue bear with both her little dimpled hands and *held it to her heart*. My own heart broke into about 847 pieces, right there on our kitchen floor. I plopped down on the hardwood and pulled her into my lap. After a few minutes of snuggles and a butterfly kiss, she had returned to her sunny self and scampered off for another adventure. My Momma-heart grew a bit wiser that day. And I had learned something precious and invaluable about our dear little daughter. In her chest beats one of the most sensitive and tender hearts I've ever met. Ever.

And I must take that into account in the ways in which I teach and train her. In our family, we've had very determined tots and very easy-to-guide young-sters. We've worked with children in the midst of the "terrible twos" who test every. single. boundary. daily. But nothing about these experiences needs to be "ter-rible." It's beautiful!

When children reach the stage that they question rules and test limits, they are developing a character that is uniquely their own. They are seeking guidance from Momma and Daddy in the only way they know how. By acting in ways that Mommas see as defiance, they are simply using their baby language to ask:

"Are you going to take my hand and lead me 'in the paths of righteousness for His name's sake (Psalm 23)?' Will you teach me how to grow the fruits of self control and gentleness in my life? Do you love me enough to see this through?"

Children are like a delicate souffle. We've all heard the stories of disastrous souffles that fell sorrowfully flat, just at the height of anticipation! For many, the first failure forces them to retreat and never try the souffle again—it's too risky and difficult, and failure is just plain painful. For other home cooks, it instills a determination to master the craft of the souffle. It's these resolute souls that see the lightly browned tops of their souffles reach for the sky, standing tall and lovely—sometimes after their second or third or fourth try! It is then that these same cooks proclaim how truly easy the souffle is to make, once you've practiced each step and are able to recognize the details of the ingredients and their preparation.

Our children need for us to learn the ingredients that make up their tiny hearts. A Momma needs to take the time to learn the delicate tendencies of the souls of her children, so that she can shepherd them gently—to help them to rise tall! Boundaries in the life of a child show them without words that we love our children too much to leave them to themselves to figure out how to grow up. The Bible teaches that a child left to himself brings his mother to shame

(Proverbs 29:15). We need to pray that the Lord would bless us with the determination to raise our babies with one eye on His Word and the other on the delicate ingredients of our children. Every Momma falls on her nose. Many times. But when we are driven by a persevering heart, fueled by the Lord alone, we can scrape ourselves back up from our parenting failures and try once again.

When a souffle falls in the middle, savvy chefs create a delicious sauce to pour into the hole, so that the already tasty souffle is now filled with extra tastiness! Maybe even hand-whipped cream with chocolate shavings. A bonus treat-within-the-treat! We need to see our "failures" as an opportunity to fill ourselves—and our children—with even more wholesome goodness that only comes from Him.

Babies need Mommas who won't give up on them when they have difficult days. Babies need Mommas who will carefully watch the makings of their hearts, helping them to cull the selfishness and the whininess and planting the seeds of grace and gentleness. Babies need Mommas who will help them to guard their hearts, for out of our hearts grow the true stuff of life (Proverbs 4:23).

Psalm 134 paints an amazing picture of how well the Lord knows each and every one of us. He has created us in the womb of our mothers! His mighty hand has stitched together the most delicate of all "ingredients": He has united the body that He has made with the soul He created to inhabit it. He knows our quirks and our eccentricities. He knows our strengths and our foibles. And still He loves us, giving us the grace to be who He made us to be. We need to display this same sort of love to our babies.

Christian Mommas need to be studiers of the hearts of our children. We need to discover what they're "made of" and point them to the Lord—praising Him for their strengths, that they might bring glory to Him! And praising Him for their weaknesses, that they might be used to bring glory to Him as well (2 Corinthians 12:9).

Every baby is unique. One-of-a-kind. Just like every Momma is one-of-a-kind. He has chosen just the right baby for you! He paired you and your baby at the beginning of time, when the foundation of the earth was laid. And He chose you, Momma, to raise the sweet child He placed into your arms. He knows the "mix" that will result when your hearts are stirred together. And as your baby grows and you fold your lives together, determine to fix your eyes on Him so that you might rise tall together to sing His praises.

Love (Your Baby) *Notes*

Allow your baby's personality to shine! Not all babies will be interested in crawling at seven months. Not all babies will love bath time. Not all babies like to interact with strangers. The Lord made your baby unique. Give your baby the grace to be who God made him or her to be.

9

Fair Weather Friends

Forecast the Needs of Your Baby

The horse is prepared against the day of battle: but safety is of the Lord. —Proverbs 21:31

Before our first daughter was born, I read all the trendy parenting magazines. I read books on baby care. I studied catalogs of baby gear and was so excited to find a diaper bag made by one of our favorite outdoor gear manufacturers. When it arrived, it was so spacious and well-suited to organization! I immediately set about filling up each pocket and mesh pouch with everything I might need: a travel-size baby lotion, a sample-size diaper cream, nursing pads, change of clothes for the baby . . . the list goes on and on. I was so well prepared! Or so I thought.

Our firstborn was a marvel in the diapering department. She would have a bowel movement only about once every five days or so. This frightened me terribly at first, but our wise family doctor pointed out that everything was working fine—and as a breastfed baby, her body was super-efficient at using all it took in. My nerves were put at ease, and I simply prepared for the inevitable giant-sized diaper filling that came on a weekly basis. Interestingly enough, her favorite place to "go" was in her car seat.

When our baby was about 3 months old we were at church, and our precious little girl was asleep in her car seat. I began to see the telltale signs of a massive diaper filling and leakage problem. We hustled to the nursery, and my fears were confirmed. The mess was everywhere. Oozing from the baby's diaper onto the changing table. On her undershirt. On her dress. On my shirt. On my skirt. All over the poor girl's tummy and back . . . Every mother has experienced just such a blowout. I went for my trusty carryon suit-case-sized, filled-to-the-gills-with-enough supplies-to-last-any-small-baby-for-a-month-diaper-bag and . . . I had forgotten to bring it to church. I was left to scrounge around the nursery for anything I could find, and that happened to be a size five diaper (intended for a 30-pound baby) and a few dried-out wipes that only worked when I added water to them.

My sweet baby smiled at me, and her brown fawn eyes sparkled, even though she was dressed in a diaper that was fastened up around her armpits when I buckled her into her car seat (that did not escape the mess and needed to be laundered). She didn't care that this tiny empress had no clothes. She grinned her gummy smile at me, and though my mortification was great, my heart melted at the sight of her. We scooted out the door and drove straight home where she had a bath and our washing machine hummed to the tune of sweet domestic harmony.

That diaper bag is still in my garage, though I

haven't used it in years. It truly is the size of a suitcase.
I think my three-year-old could comfortably sit inside
of it. And what good did it do me? None whatsoever.
I have since become a minimalist in what I bring with
me, and usually bring just a diaper and a package of
wipes in my purse or stroller storage basket.

Over the course of eleven years of continual
baby-raising, I have learned to anticipate the needs
of my babies and prepare for them ahead of time.
It's true that I only bring a diaper and wipes into the
library, but I leave a well-packed storage bin in the
car. I no longer travel with
sample-sized just-in-case
random "maybe" items. For
example, my current needs
bin includes: 4 diapers for
each twin, a change of clothes
for each baby, a nearly-full
package of wipes, 2 pull-on
training diapers for each of my
two who leave me very little
time to reach a restroom when
they need one, and a change of
underwear and pants for each

> "Don't become
> a fair-weather
> Momma who misses
> out on the sweet-
> ness of life because
> you are not prepared
> to meet the urgent
> needs of the moment."

of those just mentioned. There is a full-size sunscreen
and a full-size bug spray and a jumbo-sized hand san-
itizer. That's it. I restock this bin on a weekly basis, or
daily if we are away from home more frequently.
I carry a diaper bag for essentials when we are too far
from the car to reach it quickly, and we travel light.
I've learned that my focus better remains on my

children, when I have less "stuff" to push, pull and haul around with us.

Prioritizing the needs of a baby is the same as prioritizing the needs in the daily life of a family. Meals need to be prepared. Dessert is optional. Bathrooms need to be scrubbed on a regular basis. Vacuuming under the sofa cushions is optional. Clothes need washing. Ironing is optional.

Anticipate the needs that inevitably arise in caring for children, and prepare for them. Add diapers to the grocery list when you break the seal on the last package from the closet. Purchase next year's spring clothes when they go on clearance this year. If it looks like rain on the day your family has planned to play at the park, pack rain coats and puddle boots and jump right in! Don't become a fair-weather Momma who misses out on the sweetness of life because you are not prepared to meet the urgent needs of the moment.

The Lord has done this for us in the grandest sense of all: He sent Jesus to die for our sins, so that we might live eternally with Him! He knew of our need way back in the beginning, and He prepared a way to meet that need. God knew our souls would be sick and dying, and He sent His Son to bring health and life. But He also realizes that our bodies need to be cared for while on earth. Our own little mission field sits around our dinner tables every evening, and our children need to know that we are doing our best to meet their physical needs as well as their spiritual needs (James 2:14-17).

Christian Mommas must realize that after God and our marriages, the care and nurture of the souls of our children is the topmost priority, and our hearts and minds should continually be tracking along this line. But we must recognize that our babies come to us in a body of flesh that requires much care. As it says in James, in order to effectively share our faith with others, we must consider and meet their physical needs before their ears and hearts can be open to the Gospel. When our babies are not worried about their hungry bellies or soggy diapers, they will be much better able to hear what our hearts are whispering.

We make our lives easier and their lives happier when we anticipate the needs of our babies and prepare for those needs ahead of time. Caring for their needs well enables our babies to soak up truth.

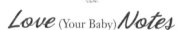

Love (Your Baby) *Notes*

Become a forecaster of needs in the life of your baby. Be prepared for needs before they arise, and don't be taken by surprise when life doesn't go as planned… because it won't go as planned.

10

Memory Lane

Record the Moments of
Love and Laughter

I will open my mouth in a parable: I will utter dark
sayings of old: Which we have heard and known and
our fathers have told us. We will not hide them from
their children, shewing to the generation to come
the praises of the LORD, and his strength, and his
wonderful works that he hath done . . . That the gen-
eration to come might know them, even the children
which should be born; who should arise and declare
them to their children: That they might set their hope
in God, and not forget the works of God. . . .
—Psalm 78:2-7

Every year, the Lord shows His mighty strength in
the utterly breathtaking storms He creates and
disperses across the lands. The news media reports
endlessly on the magnitude and destruction of these
storms, holding microphones beneath the noses of
dazed people who have lost loved ones and possessions in the literal blink of an eye. The media frenzy
turns to other news after a few days, but those left to
live in the wake of a storm work for years to rebuild

the lives they lived prior to the few moments in history that blew everything away.

Two years ago, just such a storm barreled down a peaceful valley in the southern United States. A dear, God-fearing family who seeks to honor the Lord in all they do, found themselves huddled together in their basement as a tornado blew away the house that stood above them. In a very few moments, all of their earthly possessions and their home itself, were gone. God was gracious and spared their lives, but the rebuilding has lasted for years. The Lord is faithful, and He has blessed them with a new and sturdy home, built with many parts made from the trees felled by the tornado. This family is a living testimony to the fact that the Lord can and does exchange beauty for ashes!

Few of us will ever live through such a dramatic event as standing by while our home is wiped away. But all of us lose precious pieces of ourselves—and our family's history—to a silent and irrevocable eraser: the passage of time.

When I was a freshly-minted mother, happily absorbed in the early stages of motherhood, I remember being quietly appalled at wise and aged mothers who could not remember the basics of their children's babyhoods.

"How much did your baby weigh at birth? What was her first word? When did you begin to feed her solid foods, and what did you give her?" Many mothers I spoke with simply did not remember these details. I was truly shocked, and I began to write a journal for my new baby that described all these firsts, in detail, for her to read "someday."

Ah, the passage of time. Now that I have a few more years of mothering to my name, I realize that I did a wonderful thing in beginning those journals for our babies, but I did so for all the wrong reasons. I was like a bride who spends a year planning the perfect wedding day: flowers, gowns, appetizers and entrée, cake, punch, candles . . . but never understanding that preparing for the *marriage* is infinitely more important than the components of the wedding itself.

Will my babies ever care what they weighed at birth? They might. Will my children wish to know my heart and its endless love for them? Of course they will. And even more important than that, they need to know the everlasting love the Lord has for them, and all the ways He has shaped, molded, and pruned their lives—even before they were aware of His fingerprints on every single day of their existence. My journal entries have changed since those early days. They are fewer and farther between, but much more meaningful. They are filled with the aroma of Christ in the lives of our children.

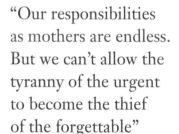

"Our responsibilities as mothers are endless. But we can't allow the tyranny of the urgent to become the thief of the forgettable"

Part of our jobs as Christian Mommas is to be a "rememberer" for our children. We need to remember what the Lord has done! So often, when I read about the Israelites and their flubs and blunders and disbelief in the desert, I become frustrated with them. The Lord is literally before their faces! He is visibly leading them, and they won't believe! They won't listen! They simply won't obey! They have forgotten God's good works, and rather than rely on His unfailing faithfulness, they grumble and stew and moan in a "woe-is-me" fashion. They are . . . *me*. It is all too easy for me to forget that the Lord has carried me through the difficult times in the past. When life gets hard and I'm exhausted and overwhelmed, I forget that God has chosen this circumstance to shape me. To shape me to look more like His Son.

Another and equally important job as that of rememberer, is that of storyteller. Not only must we remember our family's history (which as we all know is simply His-story), but we must tell that story to our children. Remember the generation that followed Joshua? The same Joshua who walked with Moses and led the people of Israel into the Promised Land? When Joshua and all of his generation had died, the next generation—the very next generation! "knew not the Lord, nor yet the works which he had done for Israel" (Judges 2:10). God had saved the Israelites from slavery, fed and clothed them in their desert wanderings, led Joshua and his armies throughout the Promised Land, and blessed his people abundantly . . . but their children forgot their God and all He had done for them.

We need to use every tool that the Lord has given us to make sure that we've done our part to impress upon the hearts of our babies all of what the Lord has done, so they might grow up knowing His works, seeing His shaping of Creation and hearing His whisper. Part of this is keeping a record of the milestones in life, and the other part is sharing that record again, and again, and yet again.

Life can feel like a whirlwind when there are half a dozen little mouths to feed and a dozen little feet to shoe. Two bathrooms to scrub and eight loads of laundry to fold. Thirty-six math problems to check and a hundred and twenty fingernails and toenails to trim. A dog to walk and a yard to mow. Our responsibilities as mothers are endless. But we can't allow the tyranny of the urgent to become the thief of the forgettable. We must make sure that in the bluster of our days, we pause long enough to remember. Remember the big events and the small. The adorable and the hilarious. The cute mispronunciations and the majesty of a beautiful sunset. A baby's first steps and a daughter's baptism. A son's first prayer and a father's tender leading.

Remember what God has done. Write it down. And rejoice with your children in seeing the work of the Lord in their lives from their very earliest moments.

Love (Your Baby) *Notes*

Record the sweet and the difficult moments in life. Keep a journal of milestones, and purpose to write in it at least twice yearly. Keep a calendar on the wall for the daily memory-keepsakes and cute quotes once your baby is talking.

11

Read with Your Baby

Lessons on Life

In the beginning was the Word, and the Word was
with God, and the Word was God . . . In him was
life; and the life was the light of men. —John 1:1 & 4

Reading is a sensory activity. Sight: words on the
page, splashes of color in an array of artistic media.
Sound: listening with delight to a book being read
aloud, learning to sound out and decipher what all
those squiggly lines "say." Touch: the feel of a book in
the hands; its weight, its texture, the relative fragility of
the pages. Smell: does anything compare to the aroma
of an old book? Taste: delicious; just ask any baby who
is mobile enough to get her hands on a book.

Ours is a family of book lovers. There are books
on every imaginable surface in our home. Shelves line
our "couch" room and the books are nearly spilling
over onto the floor. Every child has a bookshelf next
to his or her bed. My husband and I have books lining
our own bedroom. We have one whole shelf devoted

to library books, and that is filled to the brim.

Dusty. A bit disorganized. And invaluable.

One of our daughters' all-time favorite books is *The Princess and the Kiss* by Jennie Bishop. It's all about a young lady who recognizes the God-given gift of her first kiss, and how she meets and evaluates suitors. She studies the character of each man and weighs in her heart whether she can trust each man with her treasured kiss. She keeps her kiss safe until she finds a man that will love and cherish it—and her—with all his heart. What a sweet story!

Whenever the grandparents come for a visit, our children each wobble towards them with a stack of books on their arms they can barely see over, and they plunk into the laps of Grandpa or Grandma and snuggle in (because *everyone* knows that's the *only* way to really enjoy a book!), ready for a long stay of reading. Such was the case with *The Princess and the Kiss*. My father began to read to the girls, and they sat, enthralled for the first few pages, even though they had heard it eleventy-seven times before. My dad turned to the first suitor page and my girls looked up, jolted out of their reveries.

"You have to use voices, please, Grandpa," they chorused.

"Voices?" he asked, with eyebrows arching up his forehead.

"Yes, *voices*." My dad peered at me over the rims of his reading glasses with a question etched in his features. I grinned a bit sheepishly, and stretched out on my belly on the floor next to the little group. In my best Texas-drawl, I read the words of the first suitor. My girls clapped delightedly. In our rendition, the next suitor, Prince Romance, hails from France.

The third suitor is from England. My father's smile stretched broader with each best-effort try at the accents, and by the end of the book, he could see why my daughters requested the dramatic effect of "voices," even if my "voices" weren't exactly true to their region of origin.

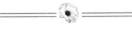

"We teach our children to read so they will be able to search and know the heart of God."

We teach our children to read not only so they can explore new and far-off worlds. Not so they can learn new skills. Not to pack their brains full of facts so they can win at trivia question-answer games. Not so they can become so knowledgable that they can teach their younger siblings. Not even to get them accepted into fine universities.

We teach our children to read so that we can use fictional characters as examples of real-life behavior we want them to emulate or avoid. We read to teach them how to discern truth and fiction. We teach them to read so they can understand how to critically analyze information and weed out that which is pure and true, and that which is rotten at the core. *We teach our children to read so they will be able to search and know the heart of God.*

Our children need to read His Word so they can pick out His Voice from among the barrage of voices they will hear throughout their lives in the media, in books, in friends and in churches. We read His Word to our children—and ourselves!—to find the steps to take in our lives to keep us on the narrow path, like Bunyan's Pilgrim. We read His Word to learn the areas of our lives that need pruning, and need it badly. We read His Word so we might know His Son, and try to mold our lives after His own. We read His Word so that our lives might be the candle on a hill that cannot be hidden (Matthew 5).

The very first words of the Gospel of John point us in the right direction: to the Word. Jesus was the very Word Himself! This verse is so dear to my heart. It is a beautiful union between Old Testament and New, of Creation and Messiah. There are those who try to discard the Old Testament as an ancient anthropological textbook. But the first verse of John shows how seamlessly the two are interwoven. Nothing found in the Bible is superfluous. Nothing is lacking. God's Word is perfect and entire.

In order to love the Savior, we need to love the Word. What an amazing and blessed gift! We are able to hold a map in our hands that leads to an eternity with the Lord of Creation! I've heard the Bible likened to a love letter written by God and given to us. Isn't that beautiful imagery? But it is not complete. If Jesus was the Word, as it says in John, the Lord sent not just a love letter, but His very own Son so that we might know and love Him in our very inmost being.

Our babies need to be filled with the Word from their earliest days. Wouldn't it be wonderful if they could say as adults, "I can't remember a time when our family did not read the Bible together daily."? We can include our babies in our personal reading of the Word; it would benefit ourselves and them! We can memorize verses with them. We can sing Scripture while we cook or fold laundry. We can write God's Word on the very walls of our homes!

If the Bible is to be the foundation of our lives as Mothers, *we need to know what it says*. If the Word is going to be the stepping stone for our babies as they grow, and their guiding light when they are grown . . . *they need to know what it says*.

And may God add His blessing to the reading of His Word!

Love (Your Baby) *Notes*

Every child, no matter the age, benefits from snuggly reading time. What a wonderful place for your baby to learn about the Lord, friendship, right and wrong, and a myriad of other life lessons.

12

Little White Lies

Lead to Little Liars

*But speaking the truth in love, [we] may grow up
into him in all things, which is the head, even Christ.
—Ephesians 4:15*

*Then said Jesus to those Jews which believed on him,
If ye continue in my word, then are ye my disciples
indeed; And ye shall know the truth, and the truth
shall make you free. —John 8:31-32*

When I was a child, I did not often speak untruth.
I remember side-stepping the truth some, or "selective truth telling," which is, in fact, not truthful. But I can only recall flat-out lying just one time.

I was about ten years old, and having a snack after school when the phone rang. My parents were tending to their small business, so to be helpful, I answered the phone. I was well-practiced, as a large portion of their business is conducted over the phone. This call came through on the personal family line, and I had no hesitation in picking it up.

"Hello?" I answered.

"Hello, who is this?" replied a female voice.

"I'm Katie," I said. "May I ask who is calling?"

"It's Mrs. G____. Is your mother available?" asked the woman, in a very curt tone.

"Not at the moment. Can I take a message?"

"Yes. Get a pencil and paper. You will need to write this down," answered the woman crisply. Something in the caller's frosty, bossy tone had stiffened my neck. I felt as though a complete stranger had no right to tell me what to do. I held my breath for a moment, but did not put down the receiver. I did not pick up a pencil. I did not fetch paper. I sat and estimated the amount of time it would take for me to gather those supplies, then said into the phone,

"Okay." The woman gave a lengthy message, and I mentally recorded her name. My mom would be able to look up her number, I figured. I only half listened to the rest of her message, reasoning that she could relay it to my mother herself when she spoke with my mom directly.

"Did you get that?" she asked briskly.

"Uh-hmm." I said casually.

"Read it back to me." She didn't ask it as a question. She had issued a challenge, and I could not meet it. I felt my face redden and my breath caught in my throat. My heart began pounding and I knew the gig was up.

"Oh . . . I uh, I didn't . . . um . . . write it down," I fumbled the words.

"I thought so. Go get a pencil," repeated the icy tones. This time, I did. And I was able to read the message back to the lady on the other end after she repeated her message a second time. I was so entirely mortified, I thought I would melt through the floor. And then I had a stomachache thinking about having to relay this entire story to my mother. Needless to say, it was a very uncomfortable afternoon for a little girl named Katie. And she had learned a valuable lesson that has never left her: Always, always tell the absolute truth.

My husband and I have done everything we could to make sure that speaking only truth—to each other and our children—would be a foundational element for our family. We don't "forget" to tell each other all that needs to be shared. We don't hide difficult truths from our children. We try our best to give them age-appropriate information that satisfies their hunger for knowledge without robbing them of their innocence.

From the beginning of our parenting journey, we have told our children the truth. When they would cry because they wanted another cookie, we never told them that there were no more—two are enough for now. Period. When a thunderstorm shook the house and made them quake in their beds, we never made up stories about the angels in heaven bowling. Babies do not come from storks. Santa is make-believe. Our goal from the beginning is to make sure our babies know they can come to us with any question—any question—and know they will receive a truthful answer from their parents.

Has this led to some uncomfortable moments? You had better believe it! But I've found that the discomfort is entirely on my part. As my husband and I work to keep the communication lines between us and our children open, our little ones come to us with misunderstandings and questions without embarrassment. Any topic of conversation is fair game, as long as it is handled respectfully and reasonably. To date, our children have not taken advantage of us in their quest for knowledge. They have not tried to trap us in a corner, speaking of a questionable topic hoping to see us blush. I think they are grateful that they can rest knowing that they will receive from us the information they are seeking without their parents giving them "the runaround."

Trust is established between two people based upon past history of speaking truth and acting upon what is said. We need to teach our babies from their earliest days that when we speak to them, we will do our very best to make sure we are not whitewashing a falsehood to avoid a temper tantrum or hurt feelings. Although it isn't stylish anymore, we need to be women of our word. Trustworthy, with minds set on that which is right and good (Philippians 4:8).

We live in a world in which ungodly behavior is lauded, while quiet, wholesome lives are viewed with distain. Untruth and unfaithfulness are bantered about on television and on the Internet as fodder for comedy or drama. As we do what we can as parents to shield our children from the worst that media has to offer, we need to be ready to talk about the ugly things of this world when they ask about them. When tragic events unfold in world or national news, we can and should talk about it around the dinner table. When a family member is very sick or injured, we need to discuss it. When a friend finds his family sadly dissolving due to divorce, we have to be prepared to explain it to our children.

But the key is to speak truth in love (Ephesians 4:15). It sounds so simple, but it can be so difficult to live out! And while our children need to know the truth, we must be cautious to not create self-righteous and judgmental little Pharisees out of them. That scantily clad woman on the billboard advertising plastic surgery? Yes, she is immodest, but she probably doesn't know the Lord. She doesn't understand that God has made our bodies, just as they are. He loves us and asks us to care for those bodies, but we should not make an idol out of this shell that covers who we really are, and only He can shape and rework our souls . . . that is the transformation we should be seeking. We need to teach our children to pray for those who don't know the Lord, that the scales might fall from their eyes and they can begin to walk in the truth.

If we offer "white lies" to our babies when they are small, why should they believe we will tell them the truth when their questions really begin to matter? Why should they believe us to tell the truth about the Lord and the eternal life that can be found in Him, if we've never given them truthful answers about insignificant issues such as extra dessert or how one man can deliver presents to every child in the world in one night? If our children can't believe us when they ask small questions, why should they believe us when they ask the big ones? Even worse, what if they stop asking us altogether because they can't count on a truthful answer? Why should *they* tell the truth when it's their turn to answer questions?

Building a relationship of trust involves a continuous sowing of the seeds of truth. As we walk that narrow path with our children, first holding them up as toddlers, then watching them venture forth on their own—we can expect to see the fruit of those seeds. It will ripen in the form of children who choose to tell the truth, even when it's difficult, even when they might have privileges removed for doing so.

Speaking the truth is sometimes difficult, but it is always the right thing to do. When we teach our children to tell the truth, and model it for them, they can live having confidence in their Mommas. Freedom is found in truth (John 8:32). And when we've taught our children to speak the truth even—especially—concerning their own shortcomings, they will have confidence in God's forgiveness and the freedom that comes in living life with a clear conscience before the Lord.

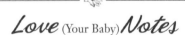

Love (Your Baby) *Notes*

Always tell the truth. Teach your baby that he or she can always come to you for the absolute truth, no matter what. Don't tell your baby that the ice cream is "all gone" when it's not. Building trust is a two-way street; you need to model trustworthy behavior to raise a trustworthy child.

13

Smile

Like You Really Mean It

And God said, 'Let us make man in our image, after our likeness. . . .' —Genesis 1:26

The Lord bless thee, and keep thee, The Lord make his face shine upon thee, and be merciful unto thee, The Lord lift up his countenance upon thee, and give thee peace. —Numbers 6:24-26

Family photos. At each year's end, our mailbox fills to the brim with the smiling faces of our family members and dearest friends dressed in sweaters or their Sunday best. We display these photos for months, long after the calendar has flipped to a new year. It's such a joy to watch the faces of new babies being added to the yearly portraits, and the toddlers growing, year by year into teens.

Sometimes, these same toddlers are not altogether thrilled to be included in the family photo. With eight busy, bustling, joyful children to cluster and snap . . . our photos have captured interesting faces upon the countenances of the youngest members of our family. Often, the two to four-year-crowd pouts dramatically, arms crossed with lower lip protruding for the camera. This is followed by all manner of hilarity and silly antics performed by Daddy and Momma, trying to coax a smile from this younger set. All the while, the older children have a decidedly frozen and emotionless "cheesy grin" that doesn't come close to resembling their usual bright-eyed smiles. The "cheesy grin" can look like a grimace. It can look like that poor child is in pain.

All that to say, we are thankful for digital photo retouching software.

> "…our true natures—our heart of hearts—will daily be revealed to our children with all the blisters, scars, and pimples exposed."

We truly enjoy studying the faces of friends and relatives, children and adults, exclaiming, "She looks just like Auntie!" or "Isn't he growing up to be the spitting image of his dad?" Just as a child's physical appearance may resemble his father or mother, so does his personality.

It's been said that children reflect the character of their parents in broader and bolder brushstrokes. Essentially, that means that our true natures—our heart of hearts—will daily be revealed to our children with all the blisters, scars, and pimples exposed. A humbling thought. Consider, then, that what they see, they will mimic; usually in an exaggerated fashion. Very humbling, indeed.

As Christians, our heart of hearts should be the new creation that God has promised to give us through His Son (2 Corinthians 5:17). God has chosen to make us in His own image! As His children, we are to reflect His nature. In turn, our children reflect our own nature . . . and hopefully, the Lord's.

The Lord loves His children (John 3:16). The Lord delights in His children (Psalm 149:4). He makes His own face to shine upon us, and fills us with His peace (Numbers 6:24-26). Shouldn't our faces reflect this same love, delight, and peace of God to our own children? As mothers, we are called to display the loving, servant's heart that Christ displayed to His people throughout His time on earth. We are to be a living example of Love Himself, daily displayed before our children.

When I was growing up, I learned that my mom is an eternal optimist. She has a sunny disposition and a ready smile. Her phone-voice for the small business that she and my dad built and still run instantly puts people at ease and gives their customers confidence in the services they sell. Did you know that you can "hear" the smile in someone's voice on the other end of the phone? It's true. And my mom is living proof. All over their very small town, she is known as a hopeful, cheerful, and kind lady . . . even to the point of earning herself the nickname of "Merry Sunshine." And it fits her beautifully! By watching my mom, I learned that a simple smile can create a bridge between two people who may not have ever shared a thought or a word with each other.

What is the universal symbol of delight? Of peace? Of joy? A simple smile. A smile upon the lips of a stranger can create the first building block to discovering a friend. A smile upon the face of a friend can encourage and cheer the most discouraged heart. A smile on the face of a loved one can become a rainbow of promise in an otherwise difficulty-flooded day. A smile upon a mother's face—and her heart—brings reassurance, soothes insecurities, and bolsters the courage of a child.

Babies reflect what they see. When Christ is alive within the heart of a mother, her countenance will proclaim it for all the world to see. When a baby sees peace upon the face of his mother, his own face bursts forth with the radiance of joy and love.

Love (Your Baby) *Notes*

Babies know when you are faking a smile, just like the police officer does when he pulls you over to write a speeding ticket. Smile at your baby with your mouth, your eyes, and your heart.

14

In the Eye of the Beholder

Maintain Eye Contact

Though I speak with the tongues of men and of angels, and have not charity, I am become as sounding brass, or a tinkling cymbal. —1 Corinthians 13:1

We live in a world that prides itself in being "connected." Most adults have at least one "smart" gadget: phone, tablet, laptop, etc. We are constantly being interrupted by sounds of alarms (Time to feed the dog!), jingles announcing telephone calls and voicemails ("Hi Kate—got your e-mail. Hope my call helped you to find your phone. Again."), buzzing of text messages (Cn U rd ths?) and trumpets announcing the sound of e-mails being delivered again, and again, and again (Free shipping through midnight!). Our attention is being pulled in twenty directions at once, all because of the technology that is supposed to help us stay connected. With it. Plugged in to the lives of our friends and family.

But does it help us stay connected?

Have you glanced around a restaurant recently while waiting for your food? More often than not, whole families can be sitting together (dinner together is good), each one staring at their laps while their thumbs do the talking to those who aren't present (ignoring each other is bad). When we allow gadgets to become glued to our hands, we allow our hearts to become unglued from the *real* people in our lives.

Mothers are the queens of multitasking. We were designed by our Creator to be able to hold a baby on one hip, brown beef with the other hand, direct the toddler to share his trucks with our voice, shoo the dog from the kitchen with a toe and hear the buzz of the clothes dryer announcing the beginning of the Race Against Wrinkles. In a flash, we can pull the meat from the heat, grasp the boy's hand, traipse down the hallway, sit the baby in the laundry basket full of clean, warm clothes, and hug a toddler in our lap while we fold. Where does a "smart" gadget fit into this scenario? It doesn't.

Mobile Phone Bad Behavior (MPBB) is on the rise, and it calls for drastic measures. Restrict gadget time! Cut MPBB from your life!

As Mommas, we need to make sure that our babies know that they come first in our hearts, in our minds, and in our lives. When we are constantly only glancing at them over a shiny gadget, love is not the message we communicate. We should behold our babies as the apples of our eyes! And too often, we give them a distracted "in a minute" response, while we answer a text or send just one more e-mail.

Grown-ups often overlook babies. Have you ever watched adults when they are addressing a family? Most never speak to the youngest children. And they very rarely make eye contact with babies. They speak over their heads as if they are not even present. I try my best to smile directly at every baby I have the chance to talk to. Did you know that, more often than not, a baby will return your smile when you genuinely smile at him or her?

Babies are some of the best studiers of non-verbal cues of any people on earth. They can feel the tense muscles of the arm that holds them. They notice immediately if there is a smile lacking on the face that hovers over them to change a diaper or offer a bottle. Babies know instantly if your eyes are on them, but your thoughts are elsewhere. When we allow our hearts to become distracted, it shows in every feature and in every muscle of our bodies. And our babies see it and feel it. And they become troubled and fussy as a result.

"When we are constantly only glancing at them over a shiny gadget, love is not the message we communicate."

The very first verse of the Love Chapter, as it is so called, declares that if one speaks with the tongues of men or angels without love, anything beautiful that might be forthcoming is only loud and ear-splitting, like a cymbal that is out of step with the rest of the orchestra. When we finally put down our gadget and truly engage with our children "when they are old enough to know the difference," we don't want to find that after years of being second (or third or twelfth) in our thoughts . . . our children have effectively tuned us out. Just as we have tuned *them* out for so long. We become a cymbal clanging in their ears, rather than a voice of love and wisdom, guiding them through the paths of their lives.

Our babies have a right to expect the undivided attention of their Mommas. Would we ever expect to be taken seriously in our adult interactions if we never maintained eye contact with those we spoke to? Of course we wouldn't. Why would we expect our babies to instantly feel connected to us when we choose, occasionally, to make them the focus of our attention? Our children do not come with on/off buttons. They are "on" all the time, observing, learning, and surveying the world they live in. We need to reassure our little ones that they are a million-zillion times more important than anything that could flash across the screen of our gadgets.

Technology does have its place. I'm writing this sentence on a computer. I own a shiny smart phone. But God has given me a shiny new baby to love and cuddle and teach and raise for His glory . . . and I'm choosing to make that baby (all my babies!) my priority, above social networking and "connectedness." I've learned to keep my phone where I can't hear it most of the day. I keep the sound off most of the time. I have carved out half an hour in the morning and another half an hour in the evening for gadget-ing and answering e-mails. Truth be told, I don't miss *anything* I can't catch up on later. There was a time before instant messaging—about 5,000 years, to be exact—

when people spoke with each other face-to-face, without the help of miniature screens. They wrote to each other with real paper and ink, without acronyms, the dropping of letters, and send buttons. People invested in *each other*, rather than the latest new gismo.

God has given us all the "smarts" we need to fulfill His calling for us on this planet. And to conquer the quests He has called us to. By allowing a "smart" techno gadget to think for us, we are turning off the brain He has given us to engage and leaving behind a world of real, flesh-and-blood relationships for the artificial imitations. Those closest to us suffer the most from our disconnected and disjointed communication. Gadgets can be great tools, but all too often they become tyrants that steal one of the most precious and irreplaceable commodities that the Lord has given us: time.

Our babies are only with us for a very short time in the whole-life view of things, and if we spend the majority of their childhood with our eyes tracking on a screen rather than on them, we are in danger of severing one of the most precious gifts God has given to us as parents: the heart strings of our children.

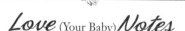

Love (Your Baby) *Notes*

Eye contact is an absolute necessity. You would never speak to an adult without making eye contact and expect them to respond to you. Your baby is a fully engaged person, just one of very small stature.

15

Joy in the Jumble

Rejoicing in Small Beginnings

Be glad in the Lord, and rejoice, ye righteous: and shout for joy, all ye that are upright in heart.
—*Psalm 32:11*

. . . for the joy of the Lord is your strength.
—*Nehemiah 8:10*

My husband and I have always had a name prepared for our babies before they are born. We pray and ponder and dream as my belly grows, and by the time we hold that sweet new baby in our arms, we are able to look into its beautiful eyes and call it by name. We have many friends who name their babies after each baby arrives, so they can meet him or her and spend a few days getting to know their baby a bit before giving that child a name. Naming a child is such a sweet gift! Just like He did Adam, the Lord gives us the privilege of naming a portion of His creation—a tiny new person! He knows and grows the heart of that baby in the womb of its mother, yet He allows us the honor of naming that bitty new being. What an awesome responsibility!

As each of our children grows, as their characters develop, and we get to know them better, it has been amazing to me just how well their names "fit" them. Like a new pair of shoes that feels like you've worn them for miles, sometimes the name of a person fits the attributes of their character to a "T." One of our children has the middle name of Joy. And it fits her perfectly! She bubbles into a room like she has been blown in on a sweet-scented breeze. Her eyes sparkle and her smile is like a ray of sunshine. She loves to tell jokes and make up her own. She loves to set the whole troupe to laughing! Sometimes this takes just a giggle of her own infectious laughter, and sometimes it takes physical comedy, such as "falling" off her chair. Either way, she finds much delight in bringing joy to others.

Have you ever wondered what moniker your children might give to you? Or what your husband might say your middle name ought to be? Have you ever thought about how easily a child is intrigued, delighted, moved to laughter? How often as Mommas do we see our daily tasks as a burden or a nuisance when those same tasks fill the heart of a child with joy? Remember how grown up and privleged you felt the first time you were allowed to do the dishes for your mother? Does that same sink filled with crusty plates and forks still flood your heart with a thrill of excitement? How is it that our hearts beat like a dull bass drum, rather than roll snappily like that of a snare drum?

Observe your baby in the next bath you give her. Her eyes will light up! Her chubby fingers will clumsily reach for a bubble, and she will laugh out loud when it pops! She will chew a bit on the bar of soap, if she can reach it, and won't be bothered much by the taste. She might crawl around in the shallow water, then stretch out on her belly to kick and splash with her feet. Then she'll roll onto her back and flap her arms as if to make a "snow angel" in the bubbles. No matter that this is the same bath-time routine that she experiences every evening. Her heart will be filled with joy—even at the sight of you gathering her towel and fresh pajamas, and her anticipation will be great.

Consider your own daily shower. Have you mastered the art of the five-minute wash? Head to toe, the epitome of efficiency? Do you consider your shower just one more thing on the To Do List? Climb in. Wet. Lather. Repeat. For the 287th time this year. Complete it and move on to the next task.

When do we allow our hearts to disregard the very building blocks that make up daily life? Just because it's a basic task doesn't mean we can't find delight in doing it, completing it with excellence. Who among us Mommas should dare despise the day of small beginnings (Zechariah 4:10)? And what beginnings are smaller than a brand new baby and all the tasks involved in caring for one?

Christian Mommas need to recognize what a privilege we have been given in raising up the next generation for the Lord. We need to realize that what we do—whether it be washing dishes for the fifth time in a day or changing yet another diaper—we need to complete the job with excellence, as unto the Lord

(Colossians 3:23). Our attitudes set the example for our children. Our attitudes fill the atmosphere with either the aroma of joy or the stench of self-pity and disdain. If the joy of the Lord is our strength (Nehemiah 8:10), then we need to show our families how mighty He is!

Babies are filled to the brim with joy. In capital letters: JOY! Everything from fuzzy caterpillars to wiggling shoelaces to the cat's tickling whiskers brings joy to the heart of a child. And what they most delight in is you. In capital letters: YOU! A half-hearted smile from you is reflected on the face of your baby with *full* feeling. A silly fill-the-time song might become a family favorite. We cannot fully know the impact of our attempts until our children are grown and beginning families of their own. Shouldn't we jump into this pool of motherhood joy with two feet? Don't simply dip a toe in or wade. Jump! Make a splash!

> "Never leave behind the *joy* in mothering. You will *enjoy* the sweetness of these fleeting baby days so much more if you consciously fill them with sweet memories."

Tickle your baby's toes while he sits in his high chair. Play peek-a-boo as you crawl behind the couch to retrieve toys. Make a bubble beard for yourself while you give your baby a bath. Listen to the ocean in a sea shell. Create an echo with a tomato can while you are preparing dinner. The possibilities to experience joy with your baby are endless.

Never leave behind the *joy* in mothering. You will *enjoy* the sweetness of these fleeting baby days so much more if you consciously fill them with sweet memories. Hugs and kisses. Zerberts on a giggling baby's belly. Tickles under a chubby baby chin. Holding each other tight in the rocking chair as you say goodnight. Fill up your baby's heart with the sweetness of a mother's love, and your own heart will sprout wings of joy. Then rejoice in the Lord together!

Love (Your Baby) *Notes*

Your baby has no concept of "cool." It's more than okay to be silly sometimes! Hugs, kisses, zerberts, and tickles are a joyous part of babyhood. Never get too busy to enjoy the sweetness of baby days.

16

A Daddy's Heart

News Alert: Men & Women Are Created to be Different

So God created man in his own image, in the image of God created he him; male and female created he them. —Genesis 1:27

In south Texas, we've been experiencing a major drought that has lasted over several seasons. Our reservoirs have been depleted and farmers have been devastated by crop losses. Rain clouds would roil up on the horizon but peter out before dropping any rain. Every single day was bright and sunny . . . usually a very good thing! But day after day of one hundred degree heat with no respite wears on a soul. During the worst of the drought, meteorologists would even report a ten percent chance of rain, just to give folks hope that rain "might could" come. So, when this spring's forecast began to include rain predictions, I dismissed them as optimistic at best.

But the rain did come. Mellow morning showers at first. Then a few gentle "over night soakers" as my dad calls them. The grass turned green for the first time in ages. Birds sang songs of joy about splashing in puddle baths. Bluebonnets burst forth in their deep blue-violet profusion, covering roadsides and medians. The rain had come! And it was glorious.

The rain continued to come. And we had mighty thunderstorms that rattled the house and pummeled the earth with hard white hail balls and pelted the windows with rain. One particular rain storm pounded the land with heavy rain all night long. We awoke on Saturday morning to find that the thunder and lightening had ceased, and the dry creek bed that borders our property was no longer dry. What had been rock outcroppings were now waterfalls! What had been stone "staircases" were now rapids! Our children's favorite play places were flooded and if not underwater entirely, completely surrounded—creating islands out of hilltops.

My first thought was of pancakes, hot chocolate and a cozy morning snuggled under blankets, reading aloud from one of our family favorites. What a lovely way to spend a rainy day!

My husband's first thought was of adventure.

After getting dressed, I meandered out to the kitchen and called out to him.

"Austin?" No response. "Austin? Where is everyone?" My gaze drifted through the windows to see our children outside, standing in their favorite digging place. Covered in mud. From top to toe. As if a master sculptor had tried to make living statues out of them—covering them completely with mud, without missing any nook or cranny. I was speechless.

Just then, Austin poked his head through the backdoor.

"Isn't this great?" His grin said it all. My mouth fell open and I sifted my words carefully.

"Wow! This is really amazing!" I answered as I cleared my throat. "You've been outside with the kids, right? Have you *seen* them?" My eyes grew large and I held my breath.

"Sure! It stopped thundering a long time ago, so it's safe," he said. "We're going to hike around the yard. Want to come?" He paused and waited for an answer. I shoved all thoughts of laundry and stains from my brain and tried to harness some of his enthusiasm.

"Okay," I said, trying to reflect his smile. He didn't notice my paltry effort.

"You'll want to change clothes." And he was gone.

We did hike around the yard that day. Up one side of our property and down the other. It's just two acres, but to our children, it's as grand an expanse as the Amazon or as wild as the Himalaya . . . depending on the day, and what is bubbling in their imaginations. We made some amazing memories that rainy Saturday morning. And our children will remember for all their days the way their dad led them on a backyard adventure: dancing in the rain, stomping through puddles, squishing through mud, digging their black rubber boots out when the muck-suction held them down. Their smiling faces and musical laughter completed a beautiful picture of shared joy and love between a father and his children.

I was reminded once again how important it is to

allow my children to experience the heart of who my husband truly is. They do not need to know that he forgot to pick up their muddy clothes from the back patio. They do not need to know that I had to wash those clothes three times to get all the mud out. What they *do* need to know is that I said "okay."

When a father loves the Lord and seeks to love his children as his Heavenly Father loves him, it paints a beautiful portrait for a child. A father's love is big and strong. He protects them from danger. He can wrestle, and run, and jump and lift them high into the sky! But he is also tender enough to bandage a scraped knee or remove a splinter from a chubby finger. Fathers teach a child to stand up from a tumble, brush off the dirt, and try again. A godly Daddy reflects to his children what the mighty love of God looks like.

And Mommas need to learn to step back and allow Daddy *to be Daddy*.

Mommas tend to run to a child who has fallen and scoop him up, cover him with kisses and carefully inspect his ouchies. Daddies will pat a son on the back and say, "That'll make a nice scar, Son." Mommas holler for their children not to climb so high into that tree! Daddies shout hello to their "little monkeys" on their way inside for dinner, calling back to remind them to wash the sap off their hands before they eat. Mommas think about grass stains when children wrestle on the back lawn. Daddies join in the match, then barrel roll down the hill with their children.

At risk of being obvious, this fact needs to be stated: Daddies are made by their Creator to love their children differently from Mommas. Daddies don't notice messes. Daddies don't remember to sweep the floor after dinner. Daddies don't care if the bathroom is scrubbed after a day of playing in the mud. But they do care about their children. Daddies can love their children desperately, when Mommas learn one important lesson: Daddy's love for his children will look different from Momma's. And she needs to be fine with that. And love him all the more for being brave enough to stand in a counter-cultural position and love his children with all that beats in his strong, manly heart.

The Lord created Eve to complement Adam. He did not make an identical counterpart to help the first man. He made a woman with a tender nature, prone to nurture. He made man with a bold, strong will that enables him to stand for what is right when the current of popular opinion flows opposite to God's word.

A Christian Momma needs to understand that by granting her husband the space to live out the Lord's call in his life, she is showing her children that when a man loves the Lord with his whole heart, he can accomplish much for the glory of His kingdom. This is not giving a "pass" for childish or sinful behavior.* This is simply recognizing his attempt to succeed in loving the Lord, loving his wife, and loving his children as God designed him to do. When this is truly a man's desire, he ought to have his wife's full support.

Men are sinful creatures, just like women. But I think many men, living quiet wholesome lives, never feel the full support of their wives. They never experience success in loving their children because Mommas can assume that loving children has to look like they think it should. But it doesn't.

Our aim as Christian parents is to give our children earthly examples of God's love. And as fallen beings, we can never fully complete that picture for them. But when a husband and wife are a unified team of father and mother, they can give a child a clearer view of what the fullness of the love of the Lord looks like by showing different, distinct aspects of His mighty love.

He created men and women. He created them with differences. Rather than growing frustrated with those differences, we should embrace them. Allow your husband to shine in the eyes of his children. The sparkle that grows in his own eyes will be your priceless reward.

Love (Your Baby) *Notes*

The Lord has made men and women to complement each other in parenting. A Daddy will not interact with a baby in the same way that Momma will. Daddies are great at chasing, wrestling, running, etc. Let the Daddy of your home encourage the noise and chaos that babies thoroughly enjoy. Allow Daddy to actually be Daddy.

There are many examples of truly sinful and abusive behavior— and I'm not addressing egregious sin or abuse here. Shepherding from an elder or Biblical counselor is in order in those instances, as well as removal from a dangerous situation.

17

Bubbling Joy

End Your Baby's Day with a Splash

*He riseth from supper, and laid aside his garments;
and took a towel, and girded himself. After that he
poureth water into a basin, and began to wash the
disciples' feet, and to wipe them with the towel where-
with he was girded. —John 13:4 & 5*

Routine is an essential part of life in our household. I'm most certainly not a clock-watcher, but
our routine places the pegs upon which the details of
our lives are hung. From their earliest months, our
babies come to expect a bath at the end of the day,
before being tucked in for the night.

I can hear many of you in my head already: "Is she
crazy?! Why create all that extra work for herself?! Kids
in the old days got a bath once a week! And if their faces aren't smeared with mud and there isn't jelly in their
hair . . . no one will know the difference! WHY?!"

The simple answer is that I want to end the day
on the best note with my children. And a huge part of
my job as Momma is to snuggle and cuddle with my
children. Every day. When they smell sweet, I'm much
more inclined to carry out that task. Who wants to tuck

the stink of sour-milk spit-up under her chin and hug it for a while? Or the odiferous remnants of the afternoon's blowout diaper? When my baby smells fresh and clean, I feel as though I would rather stay in the rocking chair all night with her sleepy head snuggled into my elbow than put her down to sleep in her crib.

When we had three very small children, three years old and younger, I remember my mother commenting that bath time was always her favorite time of day when my sister and I were little. I was incredulous. By the time bath time and bedtime rolled around, I was usually so tired and droopy that the knuckles of my fingers dragged on the ground. When I asked her why, she simply said, "Because it's so much fun!"

I will admit, I had not been in the habit of looking at bath time as "fun." Not in the least. All I could see was mess—soggy towels, the inevitable splashing and puddles on the floor, giggles and toys, and no efficiency whatsoever. And I was missing the point by at least a mile.

Bath time is such an easy way of connecting with a child and really, truly, simply enjoying each other's company. I've never met a child who didn't adore bubble baths. Even for many adults a soak is a favorite way to rest and unwind after a day full of life and its activities. Bath time creates a moment between child and parent that allows both to relax and let the water wash away the toughest moments of the day and to polish the most cheerful memories.

For the tiniest of babies, bath time provides a way not only to offer the healthful and oh-so-needed skin-to-skin contact, but bath time is a great time for undisturbed eye contact and smiles. Following their baths, our babies are then slathered with our favorite baby lotion. After all these years, I still take a deep breath of the aroma of that lotion, and my heart melts like butter on a stack of pancakes. Think of the love that is being poured out upon your baby when you press the pause button on the rest of the day, turn your eyes to your baby alone, and simply soak in the joy of the tasks of caring for that tiny body! Touch is absolutely essential to the lives of our developing babies. The Lord has given us just five senses, and the most treasured experiences in life involve all five. This is especially true in relationship. Think of relationships like a cup of coffee:

"We should have our eyes and ears open, teaching our children to observe the beautiful world the Lord has placed them in."

1) There are the inevitable fifty-cent cups of coffee that serve only for a caffeine boost on a road trip. The coffee often tastes like the styrofoam cup it comes in. This is used only to "prop" open the eyes for the final hour of a long drive. Not desirable, but useful once in a while.

2) On the opposite end of the spectrum, there are the boutique coffee shops that mark up the cost of their coffee by about one thousand percent, and serve it in a cutesy to-go cup. They fill the smallish spaces of their shops with trendy and engaging furniture, trinkets, and music. The coffee is overpriced and the air conditioning

always makes these places too cold to be comfortable, but their goal is to sell the brand and the experience.

3) Finally, there is the pot of coffee made from scratch at home. Whether you prefer the French press or drip coffee maker, whether you buy whole roasted beans or green beans that you roast yourself . . . the best coffee experiences often happen under your own roof. First you hear the sound of grinding beans—someone who loves you woke up first this morning, and is preparing the coffee! The house is then gradually filled with the aroma of something delicious. You can see the perfect mixing of the cream and coffee, as they intertwine beautifully so that there is no longer an end to one and a start to another. The glass mug in your hands sends its warmth through your hands and arms, straight into your heart. And taste . . . well, I have to leave it to your imagination. And the best part of all is sharing that experience with the someone who loves you and began the whole process.

Life with our babies needs to be filled with this level of sensory interaction, and Mommas need to provide the opportunities for these learning experiences. We don't need to purchase a pre-preschool curriculum designed with bells and whistles and tactile implements to help our babies become the next most-famous rocket scientist by the age of eight. We simply need to make our days open to the small, routine, and wonderful occurrences that develop naturally, and pay attention to the details that should be soaked up by our little ones.

We should have our eyes and ears open, teaching our children to observe the beautiful world the Lord has placed them in. Teach them to see the hawk sitting on the electric line. Trace the white contrails of jets in the bright blue sky. Listen to the birds sing while you enjoy your afternoon snack on the porch swing. Talk about the yummy dinner your neighbors will enjoy when you smell their barbecue smoking. Blow bubbles in the tub and giggle along with your baby when they are popped by a chubby finger.

Our babies learn that bath time signals the end of the day—the dessert that ends the day with sweet interaction and an unmistakeable nod to bedtime, or the really long nap at day's end. Bath time offers an easy, wonderful way to awaken a baby's senses, while soothing their busy nervous systems. It creates a moment of peaceful, quiet interaction and it offers the chance to make beautiful memories that will last you and your baby a lifetime. And it truly is *fun*!

Love (Your Baby) *Notes*

End the day on a good note. Almost everyone loves a bath! Make bath time part of the daily bedtime routine. Make it on the shorter side for very young babies, and fun and splashy for older ones. Conclude with lotion, cuddles, and a tuck-in routine.

18

First Things First

Babies Cry Louder Than Husbands

For this cause shall a man leave his father and moth-
er, and shall be joined unto his wife, and they two
shall be one flesh. This is a great mystery: but I speak
concerning Christ and the church.
—Ephesians 5:31 & 32

One beautiful June day as I was walking from my car to an appointment, I inhaled deeply of the beautiful world around me. The birds were praising the Lord with their songs. The fluffy cotton ball clouds floated lazily overhead. The sun twinkled and dimpled and brought back memories of barefooted running through fields and hanging by my knees, upside-down on swing sets. My heart was light and joyous. And then I saw something that literally caused my heart to skip a beat and brought tears to my eyes.

My heart certainly wasn't filled with sadness. What I saw was so precious that the word "beautiful" didn't begin to describe it. The sweetness I observed was beyond words. Through the tangible ache in my chest and with my breath caught in my throat, I could not stop watching.

An elderly couple long past middle age, and well into their twilight years, were hobbling along together towards their parked car. Her hand was tucked into the crook of his elbow, and he supported himself using the cane he held in his other hand. His once strong shoulders drooped, and his muscles could hardly carry himself. But she continued to lean on him for strength and help. She had just finished a medical procedure as descried by the visible bandages, and he stood by his duty to protect her, care for her, lead her to the safety of their vehicle.

My mind flooded with thoughts of the life these two must have shared. The wedding day, probably conducted during war time. A career being built and taking off through many long, hard-working hours. Babies born during the Baby Boom of the nineteen forties and fifties. Children raised, and perhaps sent off as soldiers. The possibility that they may have buried a child together. Enjoyment of the ripening of years, and the conclusion of a career. The births of grandbabies. The births of great grandbabies. Growing old together through the irreversible passage of time, walking hand-in-hand through the milestones and marking the years together. Continuing to walk hand-in-hand until the inevitable "'til death do us part." The beauty of the scene was so overwhelming, it has been etched forever into my memory.

What was it that had held this couple together through years and generations of living and loving? What kept them clinging together into frail old age when the marriages of half our nation have been discarded, broken and bleeding by the wayside?

The only answer I know—the only glue that has a truly forever hold—is God. He is the Creator of families through the mystery and beauty of marriage. He has created the two to become one, forsaking all others. For an entire lifetime. Without His fingerprints, without His wisdom, without His guidance . . . can any marriage go the distance of a lifetime? And yet as Christians, we wonder what went wrong when life becomes hard. When the day-to-day rubs weary on our hearts. When the warm fuzzies have become moldy. And you wake up one morning and realize you have forgotten how to dream together.

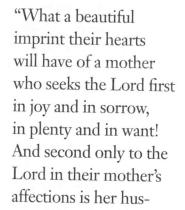

"What a beautiful imprint their hearts will have of a mother who seeks the Lord first in joy and in sorrow, in plenty and in want! And second only to the Lord in their mother's affections is her husband, and their daddy."

Day-to-day life can work like a hungry moth, nibbling away almost invisible holes into the fabric of our lives. One day, we realize that there are threadbare places and gaping rents in that fabric that we have somehow overlooked in the busyness of running a household. And yet God calls us to live in such a way that we model Christ and His bride, the church!

Motherhood is a beautiful calling, and a true gift of the Lord (Psalm 127:3). But the Lord has also called us to become one with our husbands and to model the sort of love that Jesus has for His bride—love that en-

abled Him to willingly die for her, so they might share
eternity together (Ephesians 5:31 & 32). We need to
model this love not just for the world that is watching,
but most importantly for our children who are watching with every fiber of their little beings.

We need to be so very careful that we as Mommas set our priorities clearly before us and teach our
children to do the same. What a beautiful imprint
their hearts will have of a mother who seeks the Lord
first in joy and in sorrow, in plenty and in want! And
second only to the Lord in their mother's affections is
her husband, and their daddy. What a gift our children unknowingly receive when we place before them
the example of a loving mother and father. Truly,
one of the best, lifelong legacies Mommas can give
to their babies is a pure, steady, and lifelong love for
their Daddy.

A healthy marriage takes diligence and time. As
unromantic as it sounds, we need to constantly be on
guard for the moths that seek to destroy that which
takes years to build. When we try to live out a gospel
love for our children, modeling forgiveness, mercy,
grace and love to *them*, our actions fall impossibly
flat if we can't show those same virtues to *their father*.
When we see a threadbare spot appear in our marriage, we must literally drop all non-essentials and
pour our hearts into filling the gap.

When the tyranny of the urgent takes over, it is so
easy to allow our love for our husbands to grow stale
and soggy. Babies cry louder than husbands for their
needs to be met, but a wife cannot ignore her hus-

band "for a moment," because she might find that the "moment" lasts for years and years, and her marriage needs a whole lot of rebuilding due to her neglect (Proverbs 14:1). Every Momma needs to remember that we are going to grow old with our husbands, and not our children. Children will eventually sprout their wings and begin their own families. It is the way God has ordered life. And we need to model for our children what a happy, healthy home life looks like, so they know where to begin in their own. Hopefully, they can stand upon our shoulders and surpass us in maturity and strength, passing along the blessing of God to yet another generation.

When the baby has a messy diaper and the dog has stolen the roast from the table and swallowed it whole, and the toddler has unrolled the entire roll of toilet paper into the toilet, and the phone is ringing . . . Momma still needs to go directly to the door to welcome Daddy home from his long day at work. And welcome him with a smile! And a hug! And a kiss! And a great story she can share of how the kitchen was turned upside down. Husbands and wives need to connect over the little things in life as well as the large, looming ones. Share a good laugh over a dinner of peanut butter and jelly sandwiches while the disgraced pooch licks her jowls! You might just well paint a smiling memory into the mind of your child, rather than a picture of an overwrought, weepy mother, sitting in the mess of her kitchen.

Nothing takes the Lord by surprise. Nothing! He knew that you and your husband would find yourselves out of work only a year into marriage. He knew that your house would fill up with babies faster than you ever thought possible. He knew that you would need to learn how to grow patience, kindness, goodness, and joy in the garden that is your heart. He knew all of those things—He chose all of those things for you! Life can feel hard, but growing in grace and maturity is hard work. He chose you to be His child, and He knows just what hard work you need to do to grow ever closer to Him.

One of the best ways we can raise up children to understand unconditional love . . . One of the best ways we can bring glory to Him through our families . . . Is to tuck our hands into the crook of our husband's elbow, and face the future and all it holds . . . *together*. For a lifetime.

Love (Your Baby) *Notes*

Make sure your priorities are in line: God, husband, baby. Babies cry louder than husbands when their needs aren't met, but a healthy marriage is one of the best gifts you can give to your baby.

19

Growing the Gospel

Blossoms in the Garden of the Heart

> . . . *Whatsoever a man soweth, that shall he also*
> *reap. For he that soweth to his flesh, shall of the flesh*
> *reap corruption: but he that soweth to the spirit, shall*
> *of the spirit reap life everlasting. Let us not therefore*
> *be weary of well doing: for in due season we shall*
> *reap, if we faint not. —Galatians 6:7-9*

A very dear friend of mine once said, "All my houseplants die. But my kids are thriving!"

As sad as it is for me to admit it, the above phrase has become my motto. But not only for house-plants . . . for all things green and growing. In the days of yore, I had a vegetable garden from which I could prepare almost an entire meal. I had flowers blooming in pots and beds, lush and beautiful, surrounding our house and hanging baskets that had blooms tumbling over the sides and cascading towards the patio. Today, I have a puny fig tree that I forgot to move inside one cold evening. I'm hoping that it is only "playing 'possum," and will sprout leaves again one of these days when I'm not looking.

We are just emerging from a years-long drought

117

here in Texas, our adopted home state. And every spring, I still have rainbow dreams of gardens: juicy red tomatoes, bumpy green zucchinis, striped watermelons, plump pumpkins, and of course, blossoming flower beds filled with seasonal flowers that grow and bloom from their bulbs in their coordinating seasons. Just about every other year, I take a tremendous leap and purchase plant starts. Sometimes, they are veggies. Sometimes, they are many-hued buds. But the result is always the same. I forget to water them for a day (or two or three) and when I have the sinking realization, I find my small, vulnerable plants shriveled and forlorn, way past gasping for their last breaths.

But the Lord is so very gracious! He sent me a sweet young daughter who would spend every minute of her waking hours outdoors if she could, regardless of temperature or weather conditions.

"Our actions and our words, our thoughts and our responses, are merely the harvest of what is being cultivated in our hearts. Momma needs to be fertilizing the soil of the hearts of her children, and of her own heart, with the Word of God."

This precious girl loves all living things: babies, horses, dogs, cats, plants. And she devotedly cares for any and all of these that she can get her hands on, filling her free time caring for and nurturing life. She knows how I long for the garden that I seem utterly incapable of maintaining. My firstborn is much more capable than her one decade of life would belie. When shopping

118

with her daddy for a Mother's Day gift, she chose a flat of begonias from the clearance shelf and came home and planted them for me. She was diligent to water and to fertilize and to tend, all summer long (and Texas summers can be *very* long!). Those same begonias grew to overflowing their bed, and are still bravely blooming after my dear daughter nursed them through the winter months. Although my green thumb may have been pruned, my daughter is ripening hers to fruition! And our whole family enjoys her gift!

The heart of a mother is very much like a garden, busily being pollinated by buzzing bees. When the discovery is made of a baby growing within her, the mother's heart is tilled by morning sickness. It is furrowed by a burgeoning belly. It is planted with the seeds of selflessness while in the throes of labor. When she holds that precious new baby in her arms, the fragrant, tiny blossom of love is indelibly rooted within her heart.

The love of a mother sometimes turns her into a protective Momma Bear who will fight off danger with surprising strength. The love of a mother can turn an otherwise calm and controlled woman into a weepy mess over the unkind words of her daughter's "best" friend. The love of a mother can draw that Momma to her knees when she knows that only the Lord can guide her words and her steps, and turn her heart, and that of her child, to Himself.

We mothers need to be living the gospel message every single day for our children. When they invariably fail, and we see sin sprouting in their lives,

119

we need to point that out to them and guide them to ask for forgiveness and seek the face of their Father. When *we* invariably fail, our children need to see us, hearts bowed low in prayer, asking the Father for forgiveness. They need to see us model true repentance and see us restored to fellowship with the Father through our relationship with Jesus.

As Mommas, our hearts are an ever-growing intermingling of sweet life and love. And as we grow in our maturity, right alongside our babies, the overflow of our hearts has the power to bring the beautiful fragrance of God's love or the stench of weeds into the lives of our children. Weeds can rear their ugly heads in the form of doubt, rebellion, selfishness, laziness, and countless other forms. Every mother knows her own propensity to grow weeds, rather than lovely fruit, in her innermost heart. We must be ready to uproot the weeds the moment we recognize them, or they will overtake anything lovely that has been planted.

For a Christian mother, the soil of this garden of the heart is the Gospel itself. The only way we can do all the things that our babies need us to do is through the strength and the grace of God (Ephesians 2:8 & 9, Philippians 4:13). When we sow the seeds of love and kindness and joy, that which grows will not stand in the storms of life unless it is planted in eternal soil.

Our actions and our words, our thoughts and our responses, are merely the harvest of what is being cultivated in our hearts. Momma needs to be fertilizing the soil of the hearts of her children, and of her own heart, with the Word of God. She needs to be filling the moments of her days with prayer and thanksgiving. A mother needs to live every day to its fullest for the glory of the Lord! And her children will bask in the aroma of the blossoms that grow to overflowing from her heart-garden.

May the Lord help us to remember that the relationships we tend with our children, the moments that we share, the training and correction that take place are, in fact, seeds planted in the hearts of our babies. We will assuredly reap that which is planted there. By His grace alone, it will be a fruitful and glorious harvest!

Love (Your Baby) *Notes*

Live the Gospel Truth daily. We need to be an example to our babies of what God's grace looks like in the life and heart of a regenerate sinner.

20

Lovey-Dovey

Adopt a Lovey and
Never Feel Lonely Again

Be still and know that I am God. . . . —Psalm 46:10

*Then opened he their understanding, that they might
understand the scriptures. —Luke 24:45*

When I turned three years old, my parents
gave me a large, chocolatey-brown stuffed
bear with beige ears and an enormous golden ribbon
bow tied around its neck. I immediately named him
Montana and replaced the bow with one of my own
red undershirts and a pair of pink panties. This was
high fashion in my toddler mind, and Montana and I
became fast and inseparable friends. We traipsed everywhere together. We peeked at bugs under the big
rocks that lined the driveway. We had tea parties with
water-filled plastic cups. We made cookies with my
mom. We visited the neighbor. We played with the
dog. We explored the woods and climbed trees. We
were tool-fetchers for my dad when he was working
on big jobs. We shared everything from chocolate to
secrets, and we went everywhere together.

It was only natural that when my family planned a beach vacation, Montana and I prepared for the sand and sun. We left his favorite red shirt at home, but he wore his pink underwear. I packed my bathing suit, and we were ready to go! Our flight was scheduled for early in the morning, and my family slept at a hotel with an airport shuttle to make the logistics a bit easier. The hustle and bustle was significant, but we finally made it to the beach; the sand under our toes felt great after months of seeing only snow on the ground! My family and I enjoyed the sand and sun, sampling the local cuisine and shopping in the local markets.

After a day or two, my mom realized she hadn't seen Montana since we had arrived at the beach. My dad was sure we had left him at home. My theory was that Montana was at the hospital. My parents' uneasiness only grew when I purchased a sombrero for Montana with my own piggy-bank funds. I talked about him all the way home, and how much he would like his new hat. They feared the worst when we arrived home and I eagerly sought my bear in my own room . . . and did not find him. Over the course of days and through many tears, we retraced our steps in our minds, trying to remember where Montana could have possibly been left. Our only hope was that the airport hotel housekeeping staff had found him. My mom called, and no brown bear with pink underwear had been found. I was crushed. My dad tried to console me by saying that perhaps Montana had found a home with another family, with a child who would love him just like I did. My tears only fell faster, and I insisted that Montana was *my* bear.

In desperation, my mom called the hotel a second time to see if the bear had turned up. And much to the relief of my parents, Montana was identified in the lost-and-found holding bin of the hotel! The management would not sway from their strict no-shipping policy, but a dear old friend who lived in that city agreed to drive to the hotel and pick up my very conspicuously dressed bear and mail him to our home in another state.

I remember so vividly—thirty years later!—the day my mom told me she had a surprise for me. I held her hand and walked into our living room and there was Montana, sitting on the sofa, wearing his pink panties. Just waiting for me to scoop him up and cuddle with him! My joy was great, and Montana and I remained inseparable for years to come. He slept on my bed until I went to college, and even after that, he had a special spot on his own shelf in my room. Today, Montana has made friends with my own children, and they know the story of his long journey. And they are daily creating adventures to share with their own lovey toys.

From the very beginning of our child-rearing adventure, we have utilized snuggle toys and blankets as comfort objects for our children. I had read somewhere that it's best to buy a second, identical lovey once your child shows a preference, and to rotate them frequently to equally distribute the amount of wear and scent. This is invaluable advice when your baby has the stomach flu or is potty training, and one lovey needs to be washed immediately. Or the unthinkable happens and the beloved lovey becomes *lost*. We've scrimped on the extra expense by making our own baby snuggle blankets—a simple nine-patch square (about six inches per patch), with satin as backing. I always make at least two for each baby, and keep one in the diaper bag or carseat for outings and one in the baby's crib. It's wonderful not to have to search high and low for a lovey at the critical juncture between Sleepy Land and Overly-Exhausted Babyville.

There is dispute in Mommy circles as to whether allowing a baby to adopt a lovey is a good idea. Some mothers choose not to allow themselves the added tension of having to find that one single object in an emotionally charged situation. Doctors and psychologists call it a "transitional object," and have many theories as to why small children tie their heartstrings to blankies and threadbare bears. I think it's fairly simple: We all seek comfort in stressful or emotional moments. Adults grasp for comfort in chocolate, entertainment, shopping, etc. Babies seek tangible comfort in a soft, cuddly inanimate friend when Momma isn't available. I am fully in favor of loveys for babies.

One of our responsibilities as Mommas is to teach our babies to become independent. We need to teach them that quiet time alone is healthy and to be desired (Psalm 46:10). We need to help them see that a quiet half hour in their cribs when they are worn out is a great way to refresh their outlook. Our job is to help them understand that though we love them with every ounce of our hearts, they need to learn that play and sleep time apart from Momma is healthy. I've seen how important it is for my babies to know that I'm all for them exploring and having adventures, but that I am always, *always*, just around the corner, ready to help if they have need; I will come when called.

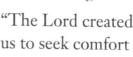

"The Lord created us to seek comfort in distress because it motivates us to turn our faces and our hearts to Him."

My babies have learned to play independently while I cook dinner. They sleep in their own beds. They have covered every inch of our living room on their hands and knees, with the complete assurance that though they cannot always see me, I always have a grasp on their location and their situation. In this way, I am offering them a very minuscule example of the Lord's care and safe-keeping of each of His children.

The Lord created us to seek comfort in distress because it motivates us to turn our faces and our hearts to Him. As Christian Mommas, we can come before the Throne of Grace at any given moment, sure of an audience with Him who truly *is* the Peace that Passes Understanding. He offers comfort, strength, and courage when what we face seems just too big (Matthew 11:28-30). Even Moses sought out a comfort object when the Lord asked him to complete a big job: his shepherd's staff. Did God *really* need to use that staff to perform miracles and show He was

127

and is the Alpha and Omega? It feels blasphemous to even suggest it! Of course He had no need of such a prop! But Moses was as human as you and I are, and he found comfort in that well-known object in his hand when he faced the task before him.

Our babies do not yet have a personal relationship with the Lord. While they are growing, learning about His faithfulness, His grace, and His mercy, they oftentimes seek comfort in a lovey. With God's guiding and wisdom, we can teach our children who He is from their earliest days—so that they will not recall not knowing Him (Luke 24:45). This is my hope and prayer as a mother.

Every child is as unique as the snowflakes that sparkle through the winter sky. Some might love on that blankie until it is so threadbare it is see-through. Some children pack away their lovies at the ripe old age of three years. For the fleeting moment in time when their hearts are soothed with a kiss from Momma and a cuddle with their blankie, it is a sweet reminder of the tenderness with which the Lord soothes and heals our hearts. As we live out this truth before our babies, they will see Him shining in our hearts and learn to turn to Him with their worries and cares.

Love (Your Baby) *Notes*

A lovey can come in the form of a blanket, stuffed animal or squishy toy, and it is a must-have for babies who are just beginning to learn to be independent.

21

Babies Are a Blessing

Being Clucky is a Good Thing

Keep me as the apple of the eye, hide me under the shadow of thy wings. —Psalm 17:8

Just after our first child was born, our neighbors came over to congratulate us and welcome our sweet baby girl. Although they did not yet have any children, the wife cooed and grinned and snuggled our daughter, and asked all sorts of questions about the pregnancy and the baby's birth. Her husband watched her and poked my husband, Austin, in the ribs with his elbow. Then he grinned and said as an aside:

"She's getting clucky!"

When a woman is described as "clucky," it means that she sees babies everywhere she goes and she begins to see all the needs and chores associated with the care of a baby as a good thing. She begins to see babies as a blessing. In our culture, babies are often frowned upon as a burden that inhibits a youthful, carefree lifestyle. God's Word tells a different story:

Babies are a blessing. A gift from the Lord. Always (Psalm 127).

About four years ago, my family decided to try keeping chickens. Austin researched for hours and discovered the friendliest breeds and the best way to care for newly-hatched chicks. Our three-year-old daughter was simply delighted the day we picked up a box of "cheep-cheeps" from the post office (yes, you can truly mail-order chickens!). It was amazing to watch as the chicks lost their fuzzy, downy feathers and sprouted adolescent ones. And it was with much fanfare that the girls brought the first egg to the kitchen for me to cheer over several weeks later.

After about a year, one of our hens became broody. She gathered an assortment of clean bunches of straw and other nesting implements and staked her claim. Of the two dozen hens we were feeding and caring for, this was the only little momma of the group. She diligently sat upon her eggs, and bravely covered them with her wings when she thought they were in danger. She was so careful, we even added a few eggs to her nest to increase the size of the clutch. The children were very kind in taking care of this little mother hen, and gave her fresh water and her own grain in empty tuna cans within reach of her nest. They had to watch their fingers though! The little hen was quick with her sharp beak and not at all afraid to wield it when she thought it was necessary.

After about a week of sitting on her eggs, we noticed that there were patches on her back that were missing feathers. We realized that she was being

picked on by the other chickens—to the point that
her feathers were falling out! That poor little mother
hen was literally being picked apart by the other hens
in her flock . . . just because she had chosen to raise
babies! Sound familiar?

Our culture tries daily to rob mothers of the
joys of raising our babies, "pecking" Mommas every
chance it gets. We need to remember that all we are
pouring into our babies—the love, the joy, the peace,
the contentment, the hope, the grace—is the foundation that their hearts will stand upon for eternity! The
foundation of their hearts need to be molded with a
generational mindset, not simply a mind that is looking ahead to this summer's vacation or next winter's
ski weekend.

Mommas need to remember that the Lord supplies
all our needs, within the reach of our "nests." He cares
for little ones and their mothers, and gently leads those
with young (Isaiah 40:10 & 11). It is our job to stand
upon the Word of the Lord and defend those who have
no voice, teaching them diligently the truth.

Does mothering involve sacrifice? Yes. Does it
involve messes? Sure. Will friends and neighbors
understand your love for your little ones? Some will,
but many won't. Does being a mother fill your heart
with joy and gratitude to the Lord for entrusting you
with an eternal soul that He has crafted with His own
fingertips? It should.

We need to make sure our babies know, without
a doubt, that they are the reason for the sparkle in
our eyes. We need to make sure they know that their

smiles are the fuel for the passion that the Lord has given for motherhood.

It is not our job to change the heart of our culture—the one that sees dimpled grins and chubby knees as burdensome, constantly ratcheting upward the "estimated cost" of raising a child. It is our job to change our own hearts into the Mother-shape that the Lord created them to fill. And it is our job to tenderly nurture the hearts of the next generation of culture-changers. The way to change our culture is to change the culture of our own homes.

Mothering well is hard work. But it is one of the most blessed jobs that any woman can hope for. Let's allow our lives—and our faces—to be billboards for the true love and joy that can be ours when we are loving and mothering according to God's plan.

Love (Your Baby) *Notes*

Each and every baby is a gift from the Lord! Our culture may not agree, but every single baby is a gift. Mommas are nurturing the next generation of culture-changers—one sweet baby at a time.

22

Truly Awe-Some

Never Lose the Awe of Your Baby

*What is man, that thou art mindful of him? and
the son of man, that thou visitest him? For thou has
made him a little lower than the angels, and hast
crowned him with glory and honour. —Psalm 8:4 & 5*

Do you remember the moment you found out
your first baby was on the way? Believe it or not,
I can clearly bring to memory every single moment
of time—for all eight babies!—when I found out we
were blessed by the Lord yet again. Whether for the
first or for the seventh and eighth, my reaction is
always the same: My hands begin to shake, and my
knees suddenly wobble like they are held together by
marionette strings. My eyes well up with happy-tears
and the smile that spreads across my face lasts for
days . . . and days . . . and days. Usually until morning
sickness descends, in earnest. The smile on my face
fades a bit then, but it never fades from my heart.

As my belly begins to grow and our older children
ask questions, one of my favorite biology lessons is to
show them ultrasound images that correspond with
the gestational age of their newest sibling.

This usually leads to digging out their own baby books, and I introduce them to the fuzzy, black and white images of themselves at about twenty weeks gestation. We often will go to the pantry and pick up a one-pound bag of beans, and while the wonder of it all shines in their eyes, I explain that our new baby is only about as big as *one* of those little beans when we find out he or she is growing inside me. Later on, we make that same trek to the pantry and the children grin when they hear that the baby weighs just about as much as the whole bag of beans. I love to watch them marvel at the thought that Baby is only as big as the dolly they push in their miniature stroller. And I love that towards the end of each pregnancy, they will ask, "How many bags of beans is the baby now, Momma?" Their wonder never fades, but increases, as the day draws near to meet our newest family member.

Do you remember with what marvel you held each of your babies in your arms for the very first time? Do you remember the first night you tucked her into bed to sleep on her own? Do you remember the first time your baby boy locked his eyes on yours and smiled? Do you remember counting those precious little toes, hardly bigger than pencil erasers? Do you remember realizing it was up to you to trim those hardly-visible toenails and realizing the miracle of life had been en-trusted to you and your husband for safe-keeping?

Just imagine! God has allowed you and your hus-band to have a part in His creation! He has given you the amazing gift of a new and tiny person—formed from microscopic pieces of yourselves! Those smaller-than-a-hair's-breadth pieces were knit together and formed by the Lord into the precious baby you now hold in your arms! This blessing of God is truly, in every sense of the word, *awe*-some!

Our culture has done great disservice to the word "awesome" by making it an adjective to describe everything from a great sale on grapes to the many-hued sunset over a pristine mountain lake. Step back from our hackneyed version of "awesome" and really allow your heart to dwell on the utterly *awe*-some character of the Lord. Even more *awe*-some is His taking you in hand to make you a mother, responsible for the care and nurture of one of His tiniest and most precious creatures. Truly awe-some.

After the first few weeks or so of mothering our new babies, the adrenaline of birth and the newness of the experience wears off, and our bodies can grow weary. Weary of midnight feedings. Weary of changing diapers. Weary of changing little snapping undershirts that have been leaked upon yet again. Weary of re-snapping footie pajamas that have been snapped crooked by a helpful, yet bleary-eyed Daddy. Weary of smelling spit-up on our own clothes. Weary of a colicky baby's cry.

We allow ourselves to think of ourselves first, muttering through the mundane tasks of motherhood and daydreaming of sleep and quiet "me" time.

Not one of the simplest, smallest, nor seemingly insignificant tasks of a Momma is mundane. The Bible says that God has fashioned people in His own image (Genesis 1)—He has made them just a bit lower than angels. Has crowned them with glory and honor (Psalm 8)! And He has trusted us, as mothers, with caring for these bitty Image Bearers in their most vulnerable moments.

Our grumblings can easily turn something that should fill our mouths with praise of the *awe*some— into something that we perceive as awful. And all because we have allowed the thought of self to crowd out all praise and thanksgiving for the awesome responsibility and gift of diapering, swaddling, cuddling and feeding a baby. It is a gift of God to be a mother!

When your heart becomes downcast, "consider the heavens, the work of [His] fingers, the moon and the stars, which [He] has ordained" (Psalm 8:3), and remember He has chosen you for an amazing and *awe*some task! You have been handpicked by the God who created heaven to bear and raise the babies He has handpicked for you! You have been blessed with an awesome job! Choose to daily, hourly, minute-by-minute remember the awe in the awesome gift of your sweet baby.

Love (Your Baby) *Notes*

Hold on to the awe. Think of those moments in life that are so precious you want to save them in a bottle—like fireflies. Unlike fireflies whose light slowly fades, you can hold that awe of the miracle of your baby in your heart always.

23

Snuggle with Your Baby

Hold Tight to Your Baby's Hand and Heart

Behold, I have graven thee upon the palms of my hands. . . . —Isaiah 49:16

I was so very grateful to the Lord that I was able to avoid a cesarean section in the birth of our twins. My doctor was very skillful and did all she could to enable us to avoid surgery, which we did. Although it took me a full two weeks to recover physically from their birth, it was a much shorter time period than it would have been otherwise! Our twins were born at exactly 37 weeks gestation, and both were healthy, rosy babies. They were able to come to my recovery room just hours after their birth, and stay with me until we were discharged the very next day.

Shortly before the dinner hour on the day of their birth, my husband left the twins in my arms, in my convalescent bed, while he drove home to gather the other children for their first meeting with their new baby sisters. I was happily tucked in with our babies when the nurse came on her rounds, and she commented on what a sweet picture we made. I smiled and beamed and just looked, marveling at the miracle of two sweet new girls.

I looked down at my precious, teeny-tiny babies, asleep on each of my shoulders. My heart filled with love so deep, it felt like a bottomless well. A joy-filled sigh escaped my chest, and I tried to calm my overjoyed heart enough to catch a small nap before the rapturous meeting with the whole family. Sleep would not come, but I basked in the sheer bliss of holding two newborns. Gratefulness to the Lord was so intense, my prayers of thanksgiving seemed like flat tires compared to all I was feeling. Words truly couldn't express all that was within my heart.

After more than an hour of this sweet time with the Lord and my new daughters, the nurse came back to check on me.

"You're still sitting there, just as I left you!" she exclaimed, truly amazed. "You've sure got your hands full."

I responded with the truth: "There is nothing else I would want in my hands, and nowhere else I'd rather be."

The nurse shook her head with a smile and bustled about before leaving again. This encounter did not brush the bloom off of the beautiful rose of my feelings, but it did get me thinking. There I was, resting and soaking in the sweetness of my life . . . I had no other tasks at that moment than to simply love my babies. No housework called my name. Someone else was taking care of the laundry and cooking the meals. My job was to love my babies. What a gift! My only "job" at that moment was to snuggle my sweet baby girls.

I realized yet again that I am an engima. Folks just can't seem to figure out how I can have a row of "little ducklings" trailing behind me and still be smiling, and utterly enjoying my life. But truly, it all comes down to the Golden Rule (Luke 6:31).

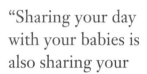

"Sharing your day with your babies is also sharing your heart with them."

My goal is to treat my babies the way I would hope to be treated. I listen when they cry and try to meet the need they are expressing . . . not simply stuff a pacifier in their mouths (we *do* use pacifiers with our babies, just not as a cork to stop up the sounds coming from their mouths). When they smile, I smile back at them. When they begin to express sounds, I coo in return. I point out interesting things to look at when we are on a walk. They blow raspberries into the air, and I blow raspberries on their feet. You get the idea. Sharing your day with your babies is also sharing your heart with them

The best way to share your heart with your baby is to actually physically hold her next to your heart. Snuggling doesn't have to be reserved for feeding times only. Front packs and slings make "baby wearing" so simple! Our babies have all loved to be a part of the action of our home from their perch in

145

Momma's "kangaroo pouch." Eventually, they grow to the point that they want to explore on their own, and I encourage them in their expeditions around the house. But every time they come near me, they learn to expect to be scooped up, snuggled, and have their cheeks covered with kisses before being sent forth on their way again. Does this take effort on my part? Yes, absolutely. But the grins and giggles that greet me when my baby comes crawling my way make every effort absolutely worth it.

"If we are asked to give of our bodies for our babies, it will never be as much as Jesus gave for us."

The Bible tells us that the Lord loves us, His children, so completely—He knows us so well—that He has our image upon His own hands. Charles Spurgeon marvels at this in his work, *Morning by Morning; Or, Daily Readings for the Family,* November 7:

> "'I have graven thee.' It does not say, 'thy name.' The name is there but that is not all: 'I have graven *thee*.' See the fulness of this! I have graven thy person, thine image, thy case, thy circumstances, thy sins, thy temptations, thy weaknesses, thy wants, thy works; I have graven thee, everything about thee, all that concerns *thee*; I have put thee altogether there. . . . " (emphasis Spurgeon's).

Think on the vastness of this statement! God, who knows every nook and cranny of our hearts and loves us so completely that He has etched us upon

His hands! Dare we compare this to the holes driven into His hands by our own sin? Jesus loved us so completely that He died for us, allowing His physical body to endure and succumb to incomprehensible pain and suffering. He obeyed His Father's command and gave Himself so we might know our heavenly Father. Because we have been called to know the Father, we can live our lives in the light of His Son.

That Light needs to shine on every step we take as Mommas. The love we have for our children should be visible in every smile, every sore muscle, every wrinkle, and every gray hair. My back *does* get sore some days when I carry a toddler in the sling. Sometimes my arm goes numb while my baby sleeps next to me, and she uses it as her pillow. There have been nights when my neck muscles feel like they are on fire after holding a sick baby for hours on end. My abdominal muscles have been stretched past recognition over the course of pregnancies and years. If we are asked to give of our bodies for our babies, it will never be as much as Jesus gave for us.

I once heard a sweet mother of many children sharing her experience, and she said, "I want to be all worn out and used up when I die!" Isn't that the way the Lord asks us to look at life? To be ready to give everything we've got and more, in order to point others towards Him? The Bible tells us that "Greater love hath no man than this, that a man lay down his life for his friends" (John 15:13). As mothers, we have one of the sweetest opportunities in the world to do just that: give our lives to our children, a bit at a time.

Snuggle your baby in your arms and feel her heart beating next to yours. Kiss her chubby, dimpled cheek. Breathe in her sweet baby scent and make your shoulder a soft pillow for her sleepy head. Sigh deeply of contentment, for in your lap you hold one of life's greatest treasures. And the Lord has given you the great privilege of giving your all for your baby.

Love (Your Baby) *Notes*

Hold on to the awe. Think of those moments in life that are so precious you want to save them in a bottle—like fireflies. Unlike fireflies whose light slowly fades, you can hold that awe of the miracle of your baby in your heart always.

24

Sweet Dreams of Sleep

Nap Time is a Jewel

Come unto me, all ye that labour and are heavy laden, and I will give you rest. —Matthew 11:28

Be still, and know that I am God: I will be exalted among the heathen, I will be exalted in the earth. —Psalm 46:10

It is vain for you to rise up early, to sit up late, to eat the bread of sorrows: for he giveth his beloved sleep. —Psalm 127:2

Sleep and the little-fulfilled dream of it is a favorite topic of conversation amongst new parents. And sleep conversations always lead to the land of One-Up-Manship. Think of the silly stereotype of an "old-timer" telling a "young 'un" about how he had to walk five miles to school every day. Uphill. Both ways! In a blizzard!! Under enemy gunfire!!!

Well, back in my day, when we had four children four years old and younger, my husband, Austin, had

to be out of town on a business trip. We were living in
a small mountain town in Colorado, and the snow was
piled high on either side of the board walkway leading
to our door. The snow formed small mountain ranges
underneath the edges of the peaked metal roof, where
it had landed after sliding off in small avalanches. The
icicles formed by the drip-drip of the melting snow
in the warm afternoon sun looked like the enormous
teeth of a child's not-friendly imaginary monster. We
were pretty well snowed in.

Austin departed on Wednesday, and our little girls
and I drove him to the airport, an hour away from
home. He used to travel a lot for his work, so I wasn't
concerned at all about his being away for just four
days. After I nursed the newborn in the terminal waiting area and we waved goodbye to him through the
security glass, we piled back into the car for the drive
across the snowy landscape towards home. I made a
mental checklist of fun things we might do to make
the days exciting ones for the girls while we waited for
Daddy to return. The excitement was to be all on my
part . . .

We settled in late Wednesday afternoon for a rare
movie night when our second-born mentioned that
she had a tummy ache. I didn't think much of it but
noticed that she wasn't interested in any popcorn.
Not long into our movie, I saw the telltale signs of a
stomach virus. That poor little girl couldn't even keep
popsicles down. And it wasn't long before her two
sisters followed suit. The oldest two were big enough
that they were able to use a bucket with consistency,

but the eighteen-month-old just wasn't there yet developmentally. All night long, I only half-slept, always listening for the cough that signaled the explosion. Every time I heard it—about every ninety minutes—I threw off my covers and ran to her crib . . . always just a few seconds too late. I would hug the beleaguered, bewildered, and exhausted baby and carry her to the bathtub. I would run a warm bath and wash all the yuck off her face and hands and out of her hair. I would then carry her back to her room and dress her quickly in the cold, then snuggle her in a blanket nest while I stripped her bed and tossed all the blankets and her pajamas into the washing machine. I wiped down the slats of the crib and the mattress with disinfectant, and remade her bed, then placed the sweet, sleepy, sick baby in her crib and covered her lightly with a fresh blanket. She fell asleep without a struggle.

By this time, the newborn was hungry, and I stayed up a bit longer to nurse her. Once she was again tucked back into her cradle, I fell into my pillow like my head was too heavy to hold up anymore. I drifted into my listening half-sleep for about half an hour. Then the whole process repeated itself. All night long. And into the next morning.

Instead of fun memories of cookie baking and snow fort building, we made memories of a different sort. I was so exhausted by the conclusion of the ordeal, that in those midnight moments when I heard our newborn cry or one of the older girls call out to me, my stomach literally lurched. I began to be so anxious about having to wake up after sleeping for only a few short minutes, that I couldn't fall asleep at all. Thankfully, once Austin returned, he was able to care for all the children so I could sleep uninterrupted for a while and untie the knots that stress had tied around my stomach.

The Lord has created us to need rest. He set that example for us on the seventh day of creation. He created day and night, and He created humans with the need for constant refueling—both through food and sleep. In our current American culture, we are used to having our fill of both. I've heard it said that food is so readily available that many of us do not know what it truly feels like to be hungry between meals. We live our lives saturated by that which is meant to refuel, not satiate. We also hear "experts" that tell us that we are shortening our life and threatening our health if we sleep less than eight hours every night. As Christian Mommas, we need to step back a bit from our cultural norms and truly evaluate the needs of our husbands, our babies, and our children and ourselves.

At this stage in my life, it is rare that I am able to sleep more than six hours each night. By the time children are tucked in and dishes are washed and laundry sorted and bills paid and e-mails answered . . . the clock inevitably is reaching past the midnight hour before I find my pillow. Austin and I have come to the conclusion that an afternoon rest is required to balance out the need my body has for rest. I used to feel so terribly guilty taking a nap in the afternoon while I knew Austin was busily working! But he gently helped me to understand that it was his desire that

I care for myself in this way—so that I might better care for our family. I realized that he would much prefer me to forego an hour or two of afternoon productivity, so that he could be welcomed home in the evening by a wife who was still capable of producing a smile.

I have learned that nap time is more precious than gold or silver. When I allow myself to "one more thing" myself out of a rest, and the baby wakes before I even have the chance to put my feet up . . . my whole outlook on life changes.

The Bible tells us that the Lord gives his beloved sleep

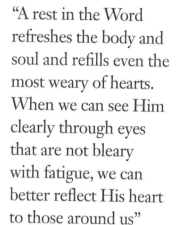

"A rest in the Word refreshes the body and soul and refills even the most weary of hearts. When we can see Him clearly through eyes that are not bleary with fatigue, we can better reflect His heart to those around us"

(Psalm 127:2). When I am run down and desperate for rest, I begin to chase myself in circles, and I accomplish little. My hurrying and scurrying is work done in vain. I lose hope. I begin to wonder if I truly am one of the Lord's beloved, for I'm certainly not getting any sleep! But I know without a doubt that this seed of doubt is not from the Lord—for there is no room for it in my heart or my thoughts when I am caught up on rest and firmly rooted in the Word. I know it's time to put on the brakes and allow myself to sit at His feet whether the dishes in the sink are washed or not.

When my body does not require sleep at nap

time, it makes a beautiful hour that I can sit uninterrupted reading God's Word. Oftentimes, this is so much more refreshing than any sleep could be! The Lord fulfills His promises, and He tells those who are weary and carrying a heavy load to come to Him for rest (Matthew 11:28). I am so grateful to see this promise and live it before my family!

Nap time is non-negotiable in our home. The older children utilize the time for reading and study, and the younger children sleep. This Momma uses her best discretion when deciding whether to sleep or soak in the Word . . . sometimes I am able to do both. It is a blessing for all of us to catch our breath and truly be still in the knowledge of God (Psalm 46:10). A rest in the Word refreshes the body and soul and refills even the most weary of hearts. When we can see Him clearly through eyes that are not bleary with fatigue, we can better reflect His heart to those around us.

Love (Your Baby) *Notes*

Nap time is more precious than gold or silver. A well-rested baby is a happy baby. A well-rested Momma is a happy Momma. Make sure nap times are structured into the daily routine.

25

Pray
Continuously

*Rejoice evermore. Pray without ceasing. In every
thing give thanks: for this is the will of God in Christ
Jesus concerning you. —1 Thessalonians 5:16-18*

*Likewise the Spirit also helpeth our infirmities: for
we know not what we should pray for as we ought:
but the Spirit itself maketh intercession for us with
groanings which cannot be uttered. —Romans 8:26*

Our only son is child number five in our little line-
up. On that first night, just hours after he was
born, with our wee little man all swaddled in bed next
to me, I lay there thanking the Lord for this child. A
baby boy . . . this was entirely new and wonderful territory for me. And I was terrified that, in his growing
up at home with his Momma and a house full of girls
for company, we would produce a feminized, nam-
by-pamby little boy who would never fully understand
how to play cars and fight with plastic swords.

In the weeks that followed, I set down the ground
rules for the girls' new brother. I told them how he
was never allowed to wear dresses during dress-up

time. We were not going to paint his fingernails or toenails. He was not allowed to have barrettes in his hair. Ever. And I prayed over that baby. I read the psalms to him, of King David's courage and boldness in the Lord. I asked God for wisdom in bringing up this little man for His glory.

And the Lord answered my prayer. I needn't have worried. Our son is 110%, high-octane B-O-Y. He never needed to be taught how to make truck noises while playing with his toys—it came naturally. As soon as he could crawl, he made his way to the girls' dolly stroller and promptly pushed it over with his chubby hands, dumping the dollies inside. He sat there spinning the wheels, amazed and delighted by the mechanism that made them turn. He loves to wrestle and romp and stomp. The noisiest toys are his favorites.

Our little man has also been blessed with his father's athletic ability. Just last week, he saw something he wanted to play with on the opposite side of the yard. So he hopped out of the pool . . . *with scuba fins on his feet* . . . and ran all the way across the grass with a great big grin of pure joy on his face. He never stumbled—not once.

This little boy rivals his oldest sister's tree climbing ability, even though she is six years older than he is. He can climb straight up fireman's poles at the play ground. He can shinny up a rope swing tied to a tree branch. He usually goes down the slide headfirst. He plays hard with every ounce of his little man's heart, and he plays with reckless abandon.

He also has no fear. Of heights. Of Texas-sized

creepy crawly bugs. Of adults who ask him questions. Of babies who are crying and need their pacifiers. Of trying to lift things that are too heavy, even for his father. Of . . . anything that I've found yet.

One particular day, after bandaging a scraped knee, and after applying a cold compress to one bumped appendage or another that was crunched in a separate incident, and after then pulling him off of some high place he shouldn't have been, I called his Daddy at work.

"It's been a busy morning," I began, then gave him the laundry list of all the adventures of his young son. "Truly, Austin, I don't know how I'm going to be able to keep this boy alive until he is old enough to make good decisions."

I was still pondering this question when I spoke with an older, wiser friend later that same week. She responded with an answer that has stuck with me:

"You can't. God keeps him alive. It's your job to keep him as safe as you can."

So simple and so very true. Every single breath that each of us takes in is a gift from the Lord. Every meal is provided by Him. Every night of sleep is a gift. Every hug from a spouse. Every kiss from a child. Every safe tree climb or swing across the monkey bars is His grace, sustaining and supporting my children.

I could live in constant fear of the "what ifs" that might befall our son, or any of our children. But fear is not of the Lord, and living in fear does not glorify Him in the least. The Bible tells us not to worry: "Take therefore no thought of the morrow: for the morrow shall take thought for the things of itself. Sufficient unto the day is the evil thereof" (Matthew 6:34). Every day is completely full of its own cares, and it's not our job to allow ulcers to roil in our bellies over the maybes and the what-ifs that could affect our families. Our job as Momma is to be confident in the Lord's faithfulness, and that faithfulness includes His protection of our families. And the best way to breed confidence in the Lord is to be in constant communication with Him.

The best safety net I can ever provide for my children is prayer. The Lord alone is the One who holds them in security. Of course, I do all that I can to make sure the bases I can cover are, in fact, covered. My children are always buckled into their car seats. They have to wear sunscreen when they play outside. We avoid allergen-filled foods for babies just learning to eat solids. We keep dangerous and breakable items off of bottom shelves stored in high cabinets. There are safety gates at the top and bottom of our stairs. But it is God's sustaining grace that carries them through one day and into the next.

The Bible tells us to rejoice in the Lord, to pray without ceasing, and to give Him our thanks (1 Thessalonians 5:16-18). And although this sounds like it is something that cannot be forgotten, how often do I neglect to do those three very basic commands? I need to be rejoicing in the Lord every moment of the day! Look at all He has done! I need to be thanking Him for the blessing of life—and it is abundant at our house! I need to be praying that He would sustain that life, that He would bless the comings and goings of our children, and that He would preserve them to long life so that they might bring glory to Him.

In the happy, walk-in-the-daisies days, it is easy to be thankful and rejoice. But we also need to be thankful when God sends trials our way. Life does have trials great and small, and He has designed them to point us to Him. And in the most desperate of moments, when we don't even know the words to pray, we can trust in the Holy Spirit to pray for us (Romans 8:26). What a precious gift of the Lord! He has provided a Friend unlike any other who can pour forth prayers for us when we are so broken we cannot utter them for ourselves.

Christian Mommas need to keep our hearts bowed in prayer throughout the day. Thanking God for the children He has blessed us with. Praying for His protection and His safety. Praying that our children would come to know Him and live for Him all their days. Praying while we iron shirts. Praying when we park the car. Praying as we sort lonely socks. Rejoicing, thanking, praying. Praying, praying, praying. Continuously, and without ceasing.

And the most amazing part of it all, is that He promises to hear our prayers (I John 5:14-15) and to answer them. Amen!

Love (Your Baby) *Notes*

Pray continuously. As the Bible commands, pray with and for your baby without ceasing.

26

A Heart Filled with Gratitude

Thanksgiving All Year 'Round

Make a joyful noise unto the Lord, all ye lands. Serve the Lord with gladness: come before his presence with singing. Know ye that the Lord he is God: it is he that hath made us, and not we ourselves; we are his people, and the sheep of his pasture. Enter into his gates with thanksgiving, and into his courts with praise: be thankful unto him, and bless his name. For the Lord is good; his mercy is everlasting; and his truth endureth to all generations. —Psalm 100

Have I mentioned yet that I love babies?

Sometimes, I just can't stop myself from scooping my babies out of their cribs while they are asleep, just to snuggle them a bit more. I know . . . you are never supposed to wake a sleeping baby. But their sweetness is irresistible. And they will only fit curled up in my arms, on my lap for so long . . . and then I will discover they have grown up. {insert deep sigh}

But for now, my twins are bright, busy, cheerful babies who have learned to expect kisses and cuddles from Momma at any given moment. And I'm trying to soak up every single baby-snuggle like a great big wash-your-car-sized sponge.

I have wanted to be the mother of twins for as long as I can remember. Since my own little-girlhood, the thought of twins has fascinated and amazed me. What a beautiful and wonderful gift! A baby is *always* a gift, but two at once! Truly a double blessing!

About half way through my pregnancy with our twins I was in the doctor's office for a check-up. The nurse busied herself with my blood pressure and weight and then helped me to stretch out on the exam table so we would peek at the babies with an ultra-sound machine. She was shocked to learn that these babies were numbers seven and eight for me, and then mused aloud, wondering how I liked the thought of twins. And I answered her truthfully that my husband and I were hardly able to contain our joy. We were simply and utterly thrilled!

The nurse then looked deep into my eyes and saw that what I said was the truth; she smiled, then shook her head.

"There was a woman here earlier today who found out she was having twins," she said. I looked up and grinned, my face lighting up at the news. Another twin Momma! Fantastic! The nurse's smile faded: "She cried. She kept saying how much work it would be. I wish she could've met you."

My heart shuddered within me, and I wanted to cry too.

On my next doctor's visit, as I sat in the waiting

room, I carefully observed the other women seated there. Most were expectant mothers. Some sat with their husbands, some were there on their own. They read magazines, sent cryptic messages with their thumbs or simply stared into space. After I glanced from one face to the next, a disharmonious chord struck in my brain. Not one of these women was smiling. Not one of them even showed a glimmer that what they were doing at that very moment—growing a brand new person!— was a precious, joyous, marvelous privilege and gift.

I'm not one to take the trials of pregnancy lightly. I am one sick Momma who spends as much time trying not to throw up as actually doing it . . . and that is all day. Every day for nine months. I *know* what hard work it is to grow a baby. I know what extra hard work it is to grow twins. But I also *know* that the face I put on pregnancy and motherhood speaks exactly what I think of the joys and trials of motherhood louder than any words ever could.

As a Christian, I consider myself to be Christ's representative on earth. My attitude and the way I carry myself speaks volumes of Him whom I associate with. Just like a call for help to a customer service desk can often make a consumer decide to leave the company when the operator is rude and unhelpful, my demeanor can put people off from wanting to know the Lord at all. What a tragedy!

We do not need to paint on happy, seemingly plastic smiles as we proclaim that our life is all rainbows and lollipops. We need to be honest with people and share that breakfast was a popsicle because nothing else would stay down. We can share that the dog got skunked and the toddler took his morning bath in the toilet. That's real life. But we also need to tell the truth in love—and make sure that our words and our faces proclaim it loudly: There is no better job on earth than being a Momma.

The Lord has chosen you, Momma, to hug that sweet baby. He has granted you the gift of motherhood. Of being an apprentice potter, helping Him to shape and mold the heart of a tiny person. Of being His hands and feet to sand off the rough places, and hold that little person up tall when they wobble on His potting wheel. Motherhood is a privilege, not a right. We need to make sure our hearts acknowledge His blessing and thank Him for the refining that happens in us as we work to raise babies for Him.

When we despise the work of motherhood, when we balk at the messes, when we frown at the inconveniences . . . we are essentially turning our backs upon the Lord's outstretched hand. And we are announcing to the world that we'd rather not accept the gift . . . or maybe we will, but we certainly don't need to be happy about it.

The Bible is full of verses that command us to praise the Lord. To give thanks to Him! To bless His name! It is impossible to be frustrated when gratitude fills the heart. Yes, there will be difficulties. Yes, the baby's diaper will overflow when you are on your way out the door, late for church. Yes, your husband will probably only laugh when your toddler manages to stick gum in her hair. But throughout it all, we can be thankful for disposable diapers and stain sticks. Thankful for peanut butter's ability to remove gum, and for shampoo. We can be thankful we have a husband at home to laugh with us in our ridiculous circumstances. Most of all, we need to be thankful that the Lord has chosen us to represent Him in a hurting world that so desperately needs to see His face.

Late at night, I will tiptoe into the twins' bedroom and just watch them sleep: their tiny chests rising and falling in rhythm with their little breaths, their lush, long lashes resting on soft round cheeks, their tiny toes poked through the slats on the crib. Then I move to the next rooms and see their big sisters and their big brother all snuggled in with blankies and bears and oh, so peaceful. Their bodies, their hearts, their minds and *their souls* are growing right before my very eyes. Thoroughly grateful to God, I stand and watch amazed through joyful tears that I have been given the gift of motherhood.

Love (Your Baby) *Notes*

Be filled with gratitude to the Lord. A heart full of thanksgiving finds it impossible to be disgruntled. Give thanks to God for the gift of motherhood, and you will truly see your babies as blessings.

27

Seeds of Hope

Grow the Fruits of Love and Faith

Now faith is the substance of things hoped for, the evidence of things not seen. —Hebrews 11:1

[Charity] beareth all things, believeth all things, hopeth all things, endureth all things. —1 Corinthians 13:7

For we are saved by hope.... —Romans 8:24

Our fourth child was our tiniest at that time by a full pound at birth, weighing just six pounds. She was so very small and delicate! I would often stare at her, marveling that one pound could make such a significant difference. But one pound on a six or seven pound frame is a large fraction of that little being, after all! She had large, clear blue eyes (the only thing that seemed proportionally large) and a head full of dark hair. When I would walk around with her in my "kangaroo pouch" baby carrier, people often did a double-take, thinking that I was carrying a doll for one of her big sisters. Why a mother with three busy children buzzing around her knees *would* carry a doll strapped to her chest, I could never figure out. But this occurred more times than I can count.

This little girl has remained our most petite daughter. Her dark hair has turned blonde, but her blue eyes are just as sparkling clear. She loves to draw pictures of her baby sisters, and she loves to play dollies with our toddler. Inside her tiny chest beats a beautiful heart made large by the love that fills it. And this sweet girl loves with every ounce of her tiny frame. She squeezes me with all her strength and says, "I love you to the moon and back, Mommy. And to all the stars too!" She is quiet and ponders things in her heart, turning them in her mind before she speaks. Sometimes I wonder what the goings-on truly are in that adorable head of hers.

One of my favorite times of the day is when we pray as a family. We give each child the chance to pray aloud and bring their sweet hearts before the God of the universe. It's so very precious it's breathtaking. Some of our youngest children talk to the Lord like they are writing a letter to Grandma: "We played outside today. And I got a dolly for my birthday. And Ezra's birthday is next week . . . " The older children remember to thank Him for all He has provided. They usually ask for blessing upon Daddy's work or safety while he is away climbing mountains.

Our sweet, petite daughter always remembers to pray for the things the others often forget. For example, as our family has grown, we have outgrown houses and cars. The other children might pray for a larger vehicle for a day or two after they have endured a long, cramped car ride, but this tiny daughter never forgets to bring this need before the Lord. She has prayed faithfully for a larger car for months, with the unquenchable hope that God will provide. She is not bothered by the timeframe. She is not discouraged when the need is not instantly gratified. She continues to pray. And she continues to hope.

Very often, hope is compared to a seed. The Lord plants that seed of hope in the hearts of His children—a seed that enables them to hope in Him, that leads unto eternal life. What a glorious hope it is! And as I have watched our daughter bloom into little girlhood, I am struck by the way her faith has taken root and begun to reach towards God with both of her small hands.

> "A mother has faith that all her aspirations and dreams for her baby will come to fruition. God has given her a faith in things not seen, namely the future, and He has blessed her with hope."

As a Momma, I think the best illustration of hope is that of the blessing of a new child. A sweet tiny baby that begins life so small that it is not visible to the human eye! But that life is visible, known, and valued by the Lord Who made it. As that baby grows in its mother's womb, her hope for its future grows as she dreams big dreams for her baby. And when that baby is born, hope is not complete . . . it's just beginning! A mother has faith that all her aspirations and dreams for her baby will come to fruition. God has given her a faith in things not seen, namely the future, and He has blessed her with hope.

The Bible tells us that "faith is the substance of things hoped for, the evidence of things not seen" (Hebrews 11:1). As a Christian mother watches her children grow before her eyes, she is given the most beautiful, tangible examples of hope in the Lord. As we watch our babies grow in wisdom and stature and knowledge of the Lord, we have the privilege to observe how they grow in love and faith and hope. Just as we are children of our Heavenly Father, growing in love and faith and hope.

Our love for God is what makes our hope in Him possible. Because without His love we are without hope (1 Corinthians 13:7). He has created an amazing three-strand chord of faith, hope and love. Of course, He declares love the greatest of these. And when love is present, it is flanked by faith and hope.

We need to have such faith, such hope, such love that our faces shine before our children, reminding them not to stumble into the sin of hopelessness. Hopelessness is a red flag that sends the message that our faith and our love are lagging. We need to weave faith, hope, and love through the fabric that is our family. The Lord has blessed us with these gifts, and we ought to wear them "on our sleeve" as we work daily to shepherd our children toward Him.

As we live before the very observant eyes of our little ones, we need to continually keep our faith and hope and love before them. Momma loves Daddy. She has faith that he will work hard to provide for the family and remain faithful to his calling of fatherhood.

She hopes the best for him and their future as a family. Momma loves the children. She has faith that the Lord will move in their hearts so they can know Him. She hopes they will be be a shining light for Him in the world. Most of all, Momma loves the Lord. She has faith that He works all things for good for her and her family. She has hope that He will adopt each of her children as His own; hope that they might share eternity together.

Just as the tiny frame of our petite little daughter shines brightly with her brand new hope in the Lord, we need to keep our hope polished and gleaming. It can't be put away for special occasions. Hope must be beating steadily in our hearts, showering its sweet smelling fruits upon our families. Hope is a gift of the Lord wrapped in the message of His gospel. And it is a gift intended to be shared.

Love (Your Baby) *Notes*

Display a heart of hope for your baby. Even in the toughest of circumstances, we need to remember that the Lord is our source of hope. We need to be the beam of sunshine, the hope that shines in the lives of our children until they know and understand true, undying Hope.

28

Follow the Leader

Boundaries Make Happy Babies

Go to the ant . . . consider her ways and be wise.
—Proverbs 6:6

And thou shall love the Lord thy God with all thine
heart, and with all thy soul, and with all thy might.
And these words, which I command thee this day,
shall be in thine heart: And thou shalt teach them
diligently unto they children, and shalt talk of them
when thou sittest in thine house, and when thou wal-
kest by the way, and when thou liest down, and when
thou risest up. —Deuteronomy 6:5-7

Several years ago, I was shopping in a warehouse
club store when we had only five children. I had
our baby boy sitting in his carrier-car seat in the
basket of the shopping cart, and our toddler and pre-
schooler in the double child seat portion. My young,
school-aged daughters held on to either side of the
cart, walking along with me.

It was Saturday—the day I do my best to avoid
shopping. But that particular weekend my husband
had to work, and the shopping trip couldn't be avoid-

ed any longer. When the whole crowd joins me, my cart is nearly full . . . before I even find the items I came to purchase. But our little children have become experts at packing the cart, making benches out of boxes and castles out of tomato cans. Our shopping excursions always draw the attention of strangers, and I've learned to smile, nod and move along . . . even as I feel their stares following me down the diaper aisle.

On that particular Saturday, I noticed a thirty something woman glance at us and smile. I returned the greeting and went on my way to the dairy section. I noticed she turned that way as well. Then we moved along to the fresh flowers, and that same woman followed me down that row too. I was feeling followed and uncomfortable. Just as I was about to make a bee-line to the checkout, she stopped me with a question:

"I just have to ask, are *all* those children yours?" She asked politely, and genuinely seemed to want an answer.

"Yes, they sure are!" I returned with a smile.

"How do you do it?" she inquired. "I can't even take my *two* kids to the store!"

"Oh, we are a work in progress," I grinned. I learned a long time ago that I need to have answers prepared and "in my pocket" for these sorts of questions. A twelve-word, thirty-second answer is plenty, and more than most folks are looking for. I have my five-minute answer for those who are really interested. And I have a let's-sit-down-for-coffee answer for those who really wish to understand the heart of the matter.

"No . . . I mean . . . " the woman shifted from one

foot to the other. "I've been following you around the store. And your kids stay with you. They don't grab at things. They aren't running and shouting. They are so well behaved. Really, *how* do you do it?"

I understood then that we *were* being followed because we were a case study. And I realized that this mother was truly seeking to understand how it was possible to have a family shopping trip without parents and children melting down into a kicking and screaming match over a box of Sugar Covered Fruity Marshmallow-Ohs cereal.

"Child training is a matter of the heart. Teaching our children the "why" of good behavior is as important as the good behavior itself."

"Well, we practice," I said. "My children come with me from the time they are small. We've taught them that they shouldn't expect something every time we go to the store. Sometimes when they do an exceptional job, they are rewarded with a treat once we are loaded back up into the car. We expect them to behave. And with practice, they do."

This lady and I stood there chatting for nearly thirty minutes. She asked intelligent questions, and I could see she genuinely wanted to know how to better manage her family. And the bottom line of all that I shared was *training*. Teaching our children to behave properly in a variety of situations takes time and practice and patience.

A momma would never expect her child to go

up on stage at a spring time recital and play a piano piece before an audience if that same child had never practiced before. Just like a budding musician needs lessons and hours of practice, our children need to practice as they learn to interact with the world. In our home we conduct practice conversations. We discuss how we behave in the library before we open the library door (no shouting, running, etc.). When everyone was tiny, we even had church practice, so they could learn to sit still in their chairs, quietly listening to a lecture on CD. And we remind our children that the heart of who we are as a family—our love for the Lord—is on display every time we are away from home. What we say to each other and to strangers, how we walk or ride in the cart, how we don't need to ask for every shiny new toy we see—all of this paints a picture about our life and our faith.

Child training takes time and diligence and consistency (Deuteronomy 6:5-8). Just as the Bible says to consider the ant, how she slowly, determinedly stockpiles food for the winter (Proverbs 6:6), we should be training our babies, one moment at a time. Before we even realize it, the moments will pile up, and we will have "stored up" much wonderful training and teaching in the hearts of our little ones.

Child training is a matter of the heart. Teaching our children the "why" of good behavior is as important as the good behavior itself. The Lord tells us to be kind, gentle, honest, and trustworthy. As we train our children how to properly behave outwardly, we also need to be tending to their hearts, and that takes more than the simple admonishments that are so often used by mothers. "Be nice to your sister" has quite a different tang than "Let's make your self-control 'muscles' good and strong! Please share your books."

All that we invest in our babies and young children pays great dividends as they mature. Training babies takes time. Training babies takes determination. Training babies takes a Momma who is willing to be used of the Lord as His gardener tending to the tender young plants He has placed in her care. Those tender little ones need outward guidance and good soil. Mommas who water their babies with that which He has poured into her will see their babies grow tall and vibrant, bearing much fruit for His glory.

Love (Your Baby) *Notes*

More training of your little one now leads to less discipline later in life. This can be as simple as smiling and saying gently, "No, no—babies don't touch Momma's earrings," and moving your baby's hand away. Diligently training your baby means they will know how to follow instructions when the toddler days of testing boundaries arrives.

29

Marinating in Grace

Choosing Contentment

The lines are fallen unto me in pleasant places; yea, I
have a goodly heritage. I will bless the Lord, who hath
given me counsel. . . . —Psalm 16:6-7

The fear of the Lord tendeth to life: and he that hath
it shall abide satisfied; he shall not be visited with
evil. —Proverbs 19:23

Not that I speak in respect of want: for I have learned,
in whatsoever state I am, therewith to be content.
I know both how to be abased, and I know how to
abound: every where and in all things I am instructed
both to be full and to be hungry, both to abound and
to suffer need. I can do all things through Christ who
strengtheneth me. —Philippians 4:11-13

Have you ever watched a cat snoozing in the gentle warmth of a pool of spring sunshine? Our
cat, Whittington, stretches and spreads his furry feet
so every single toe can soak up the heat around him.
He then turns onto his back with his feet in the air,
gradually relaxing, until it appears that his bones have

turned to liquid. Finally, he turns his face directly into the sun's rays, and filled to the brim with satisfaction, shuts his eyes.

Our toddler just turned three. She has an unwavering love for her father, and an absolute confidence in his love for her. They can be pounding nails or raking leaves. They can be walking across the yard or twisting their way up a mountain trail. They can be washing dishes or pushing a grocery cart. It doesn't matter where they are or what they are doing. Their heartstrings are so completely intertwined, that simply being in the same room with her daddy fills our daughter with joy.

"In the midst of the chaos, a Momma needs to remember that her heart can always be filled with contentment and peace, if only she remembers that her heart is upheld by her Heavenly Father's strong arms."

Every evening when he walks in the front door after his work day, our little girl's face lights up like the firecracker she is. She drops what she is doing and, with an excited squeal, she runs with all her speed and jumps into her father's arms. I have an indelible snapshot in my mind of her little dimpled arms wrapped tight around his neck, her blue eyes looking up into his face, love and contentment etched on every feature. She usually buries her face under his chin, and sighs deeply of utter contentedness. She seems to melt right into his heart. With his strong arms around her, she sinks happily into rest and refreshment and joy.

Have you ever watched the way a toddler basks in her daddy's love? A child who is loved well soaks in her daddy's presence just like a purring cat soaks in the sunshine. Her heart is filled with love, and she is at peace like a road-weary traveler that has finally reached home.

A house filled with children can be a very busy place. A hive of activity with little ones buzzing in and out of doors, up and down stairs, through the kitchen and into the family room. In the midst of the busyness that is the intricate dance of life, a Momma's heart can grow disgruntled and frustrated. Her freshly mopped floor now wears a new layer of muddy footprints. The kitchen that was clean and polished now has peanut butter and jelly finger prints covering the countertops and the refrigerator. The laundry basket full of freshly folded clothes waiting to be placed in drawers is now spilled all over the staircase landing, just like the milk someone spilled on the table and forgot to wipe up.

The path God has placed before us truly *is* lined with roses—our lines *have* fallen in pleasant places—if only we would open our eyes and our hearts to see that the Lord has provided Himself, and that is all we need. We need to direct our attention to the beautiful, fragrant blooms, rather than the thorns. He promises to give us our daily bread, and with that we should be satisfied. Our blessings abound and we need to model a heart of contentment before our children. To do otherwise would be a great disservice to them, crippling them for the remainder of their lives with dissatisfaction and even envy.

Our culture is being consumed by consumerism. There is an entire generation reaching adulthood, only to find it empty. In fact, they have stopped striving for anything at all because they have given up on the concept of contentment altogether. They have been deceived into thinking that satisfaction comes only from what they can do for themselves: What they can achieve, what they can buy, what they can build. Their hearts have been hardened so that they cannot hear the voice of the Lord and find true rest and contentment in Him.

If only their parents had shown them what a contented heart looks like! If only they had been raised to be content in whatever their circumstances! In commenting on Psalm 16, Bible scholar Matthew Henry writes, "Gracious persons, though they covet more *of* God, never covet more *than* God; but, being satisfied of his loving-kindness, are abundantly satisfied with it . . . " [emphasis mine].

Each of us are sinners. And if the Lord were to give us what we truly deserve, then we would all find ourselves steeped in condemnation. American culture today is swimming in an entitlement mentality. But the only thing we are actually entitled to is death and separation from God. When He calls us to repentance at the cross of Jesus, His grace alone—His free gift of grace!—is what keeps us from damnation. Who are we to be discontent with every other gift He has bestowed upon us?

Contentment is a choice. We can choose to walk in obedience to Christ, giving thanks in everything, praising His name with every step. Or, we can choose to feel like we should have more: more money, more land, more blessing. When we feel as though we live with "less than," we are creating a breeding ground for selfish, entitlement thinking.

In the midst of the chaos, a Momma needs to remember that her heart can always be filled with contentment and peace, if only she remembers that her heart is upheld by her Heavenly Father's strong arms. The sofa may be stained, and the car might be rusted, and the toilets might need to be scrubbed, but her heart can still sing. For the Lord has plunked her exactly in the middle of her busy household because this is where He designed her to be . . . and to thrive. Modeling contentment in every circumstance is an invaluable blessing a mother can bestow upon her children.

Contentment grows easier with practice. Just like we can choose strawberries for dessert, rather than strawberry ice cream. Just like we can choose to drink sparkling water rather than soda. We can choose self-discipline and take our thoughts captive: It's not less than, it's just different from what the culture proclaims we "need."

The Lord has chosen our circumstances. We can choose to be content in that which He has provided.

And with faith like that of a little child, we can choose to rest our hearts within His mighty one, and close our eyes contentedly—absolutely confident in

His love for us. We can bask joyfully in our Father's presence, utterly satisfied and fulfilled.

Love (Your Baby) *Notes*

Be content in your circumstances. God has hand-picked your blessings and your trials. Thank Him for His many gifts, including those thorns and thistles… because even the rough patches in the road are there to draw you closer to His Heart of Hearts.

30

Stand Up for Your Baby

You are Your Baby's Best Advocate

Defend the poor and fatherless: do justice to the afflicted and needy. —Psalm 82:3

Open thy mouth, judge righteously, and plead the cause of the poor and needy. —Proverbs 31:9

I grew up in a very small town. It's the kind of town that you imagine in a Norman Rockwell painting. Neighbors stop to visit with each other in the produce aisle of the grocery store. Folks wave at the strangers driving past as they stand by the mailbox. The community gathers around those in distress and tries its best to help when it's needed.

The flip-side of this friendly coin is that everyone feels so connected to each other, they assume that the discussion of personal trials and character foibles are fair game for community conversation. There seems to be very little that is out-of-bounds for general discussion.

My father is a very respected community member who serves on many committees and foundations to

191

try to further the best interests of the county in the tourism and business spheres, and he volunteers on many fronts. He doesn't talk overmuch, but the words he does speak are measured, thoughtful, and not only heard, but listened to.

There was once an instance in such a meeting that the group began to discuss the eccentric characteristics of a person not present. The group was not speaking in kindness or love. My dad understood their intentions and quietly, but firmly stated,

"Yes, she may have some quirkiness, but don't we all? There isn't anyone around this table that doesn't have some quirks. If you really knew this person, as I and my family do, you would find within her a heart of gold."

The others seated around the table went silent, and after an awkward pause, changed the course of conversation to something more profitable. I was an older teenager at the time of this occurrence and remarked on my dad's gumption in so boldly facing the possible scorn of the crowd. He said something so simple, but so profound:

"If you don't stand up for your friends, no one else will."

That bit of advice has stayed with me throughout my life. Isn't that the heart of being a Christian? For even more than standing up for our friends . . . we are called to stand for justice and righteousness, whether it be for a stranger, a friend or our Savior. The Bible tells us in Psalm 74:22 that God Himself is mocked by fools. If the Creator of the universe is mocked and scorned by men, we, His creatures, are certainly not above the same treatment.

Jesus tells us in Matthew 25:45 that in caring for the poor, the needy and oppressed, we have in essence, cared for Him. He calls us to care for the "least of these." Whatever you have done for the least of these . . . who is more "least" than a baby? A baby cannot feed himself. He cannot speak his needs or desires. He cannot control his bodily functions. He cannot even scratch his own nose. Yet as mothers, it is our job—our joy!—to do these things for him.

Mommas need to be ready and willing to take a stand for their babies in difficult circumstances. If you'd rather not deliver your baby to the church nursery during the service, be ready to firmly, and smilingly, say no thanks to the usher who greets you at the door. If your baby is very sensitive and does not respond well when held by several people, prepare your response before attending the family reunion (we always used a front-pack to avoid frazzled baby nerves).

> "Babies need to know that Momma is their biggest cheerleader and their biggest advocate. We need to stand up for them when they cannot and be their voice before they can speak for themselves."

Be ready to ask for a second opinion when the urgent care doctor decides to do a spinal tap on your toddler because his fever is so high. You are your baby's voice—speak loudly and clearly for his needs, and filter what you say through the light of Scripture.

Standing up for your baby will not win any popularity contests. But reasonable adults will usually not question a calm, collected mother when she is seeking the best for her baby. Remember that the Lord has given you this baby to nurture and protect. No one else on earth, save your husband, will have your baby's best interest at heart, as you do. We don't always have to come out swinging like a Momma Bear awakened from hibernation! More often than not, our winsome and wholehearted response will speak clearly of our hearts.

As Christians, the Lord has adopted us into His own family. Our Heavenly Father has our best interest at heart. Isn't that a beautiful thought? He so clearly wants what is best for us! We all stumble, fail, and have to live with the consequences of our actions. But God always holds us by the hand, guarding and guiding us . . . giving us the perfect example of how we should care for our babies. They will stumble as they learn to walk. They will have to live with the consequences of their actions. But throughout, they need to know that Momma is their biggest cheerleader and their biggest advocate. We need to stand up for them when they cannot and be their voice before they can speak for themselves.

In order to speak clearly for our babies, we need to first know where we stand. And the best place for a Christian Momma to stand is upon the Word of the Lord. We need to hide the Word in our hearts, so that our actions and our reactions are firmly grounded in truth. God has given us a beautiful and enormous responsibility in raising a precious baby for Him! May He grant us the wisdom and grace to do it well with firmness of character and a mind stayed on Him.

Love (Your Baby) *Notes*

You are your baby's best advocate. The Lord gives all Mommas a bit of Mother Bear in their hearts to use when circumstances demand it. Be ready to be tough and stand tall to speak out for your baby when he or she needs you to do so.

31

Bless You, Momma

With Bouquets of Dandelions and Butterfly Kisses

Her children rise up, and call her blessed .. . .
—Proverbs 31:28

Every wise woman buildeth her house. . . .
—Proverbs 14:1

My husband used to be a guide by profession, and that was his full-time employment. He led groups on mountain backpack trips. He steered the boat for countless tourists seeking a thrill by white-water rafting. He has taught rock climbing classes. He has helped to build ropes courses and taught staff members how to utilize the equipment safely. He has written manuals for leading groups in wilderness settings, as well as lining up the logistics to do so.

On many of these adventures, I was able to join him in our earliest years of marriage. We lived and shared enough adventures in those early years to last most people a lifetime! I'm so thankful for those experiences because I know the lingo and the needs he will have for the trips he is able to lead today. Trips these days are much fewer and further between, but it's wonderful to see the spark in his eyes when he is planning a trip and studying maps. It's how the Lord made him, and I wouldn't change him a bit.

As babies came along, my role changed from assistant guide to home-based kitchen crew. Admittedly, I miss the adventure and the time outside, but there is a special aspect in keeping the kitchen . . . it is Grand Central Station for any and all group participants. In the many camp settings we have served in, everyone from directors to staff members to campers wander through the kitchen, headed in dozens of different directions, but all stopping first for sustenance of heart and body.

I used to listen as young ladies would share their dreams of the man they hoped to find and marry someday. I used to listen to directors fret over meeting budget goals and staff needs. I used to listen to guides dreaming of the peaks they would try to conquer and the climbs they had mastered. I used to listen to homesick campers, anxious about their upcoming backcountry journeys. I used to listen to those same campers upon their return, excited and triumphant—all anxiety completely forgotten in their newfound confidence.

While Austin was out conquering the wilderness, I was navigating a wilderness of another sort: the human heart. I learned to become a great listener in all those kitchen years. And I learned the value of offering a place of respite from the world to those who are seeking encouragement, or rest, or simply a listening ear. I've often thought of how those skills have transferred to our busy home life.

Just as the kitchen is the Grand Central Station of a camp, it is also the jumping-off place of the home. And Momma is the conductor who directs from her post at the suds-filled sink. But in all their wanderings and adventures, our children need to feel secure in the knowledge that Momma is there with open arms and open ears waiting for them to return from all their journeys—whether in the blanket forts in the living room or sailing the high seas in their treehouse schooner . . . or years from now when they climb their own mountains.

Our homes should be a place of rest and renewal, of joy and peace, of growth and shaping—all to the glory of God! And you, Momma, are the tangible center of the whirlwind that is family life.

"Housework is not equivalent to homemaking. Homemaking is heart-making. And soul-growing. And life-changing. Mommas need to hold their To Do Lists loosely and their children tightly."

When the older children are pretending to be horses and "galloping" upstairs (they sure *sound* like horses!) and the babies are sitting in their highchairs practicing their vocal gymnastics waiting for their milk cups, and the preschool children are tickling the toes of the babies imitating their shrieks and yells (only louder so that they almost sound like frontier-day Native Americans at a tribal council) and the clothes dryer is buzzing, and the spaghetti sauce is boiling over, and the dog is barking at the mailman ringing the doorbell . . . Take a deep breath and realize these are some of the most precious moments of life.

Our blessings as Momma are more numerous than we can number. Sure, the days can be long and sometimes stressful. But they are undeniably sweet. We need to decide to find the fun in the chaos and realize that we can enjoy the crazy parts of life with these precious babies. They will all live under our roof, together, with us for a small span of time; we need to savor the sweet flavors that make up the blessing of family life. When was the last time you galloped like a horse, tossing in a whiny every now and then for good measure? When was the last time you tickled the baby's foot while he waited impatiently for dinner? When was the last time you sang a duet in your loudest voice with your toddler?

"Mommas can't always drop everything to play when our children want us to. But the greatest responsibility we have is shepherding and nurturing the eternal souls granted to our care and safekeeping for a time."

It's so very easy to become consumed with all that needs to be done, forgetting that the only truly important things are looking into our babies eyes while she coos out a story. Hugging tight our thanks to a little boy when he clomps into the kitchen wearing muddy cowboy boots to deliver his bouquet of dandelions. Taking the time to tuck in the daughter who had a tough day and giving her a butterfly kiss to help her to smile.

Responsibilities take time; it's true. And Mommas can't always drop everything to play when our children want us to. But the greatest responsibility we have is shepherding and nurturing the eternal souls granted to our care and safekeeping for a time. I *can* leave some of the ironing undone for now—how many shirts can be worn at one time, anyway? I *can* leave the breakfast dishes in the sink once in a while, so I can teach the girls how to weave daisy chains. We *can* eat pancakes for dinner, so I can hunt for lizards with my son. We *can* incorporate our children into our work, so that we can use those moments as shared time together—dishes are great splashy fun for little ones! We *can* leave some of the work for later, so that we can enjoy our children *now*.

If all our children remember of us is a Momma who was ruled by her schedule—Monday's washing, Tuesday's ironing, Wednesday's baking, etc.—they will grow up with the devastatingly wrong impression that housework is more important than they are. Housework is not equivalent to homemaking. Homemaking is heart-making. And soul-growing. And life-changing.

Mommas need to hold their To Do Lists loosely and their children tightly. Is it true that I may never catch up on the ironing? Yes. Is it true that I will never become adept at freezer cooking? Probably. Is it true that I will do everything I possibly can—letting go of what I can't—so that I can spend as much time simply sharing moments with my children? Absolutely. A mother who treasures and adores her babies and

children will find herself treasured and adored one
day (Proverbs 31:28).

When they grow and spread their wings, I want
my children to look back at their time in our home as
a blessed, joy-filled journey in which their Daddy and
I found utter delight in just being with them. Taking
interest in all their interests. Sharing stories of when
we were young. Connecting heart-to-heart over warm
blueberry pie. Remembering the day that each child
was born and sharing the story over and over again.

I want my children to know that what matters
most to me in life is relationships. With God. With
their Daddy. With them. Teaching and training them,
loving and living with them, is the only work I will ever
do that will last forever. Every single day is building a
legacy into our family. I pray that the Lord would use
our "everydays" to bring glory to Himself, and that we
would spend the rest of our eternal days with Him.

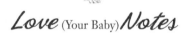

Love (Your Baby) *Notes*

Be the kind of Momma that children are eager to
bless. This begins from day one. A mother who
treasures and adores her baby will, herself, be
treasured and adored in later years. Deferred
investment, but well worth the effort.

Appendix
A Day in the Life of Kate Collins

Not all of my days are this crazy. But some are. This day was designated a library day. Usually, school work is added to the whirlwind. This particular day felt over-the-top even as it was happening, and that is why I decided to write it down.

1 am:	Wake to stop unbalanced washing machine that had been set to turn on with its timer to begin after my evening shower was complete.
5 am:	Wake to give one of the twins her pacifier.
7 am:	Wake to nurse the babies.
7:15:	Thought of exercising. Went back to bed.
7:30:	Hear 4-year-old calling for wiping on potty (need met by Austin).
7:35:	Joined in bed for a snuggle by said 4-year-old.
7:45:	Receive whispered message that a child who is way too old to have done so has wet the bed (she "had a dream she was on the potty . . . ") ick.
7:50	Pack lunch for Austin and 4-year-old who is going to work with him.
7:56:	Try to balance the washing machine that is still full of soaking wet load from previous night.
8:00:	After half a dozen tries, remove half the load and

allow the spin cycle to finish.

8:15: Help said girl into shower. Change sheets and pour vinegar on mattress. Fill the washer with said sheets.

8:30: Begin granola-making lesson for almost-9-year-old. Granola is her favorite and if she can make it her self, she can have it whenever she chooses.

9 am: Ask 9 year old to wash granola prep dishes.

9:15: Feed babies. Smell something strange . . . granola? No . . . enter dog and 10-year-old: "How much does bleach cost?" Mom: "WHY do you want bleach?" 10-year-old: "Meg (dog) got into the neighbor's trash. She had green slime all over her neck, so I washed it." Mom: (Ick!! Gag!!) "Did you wash the whole dog?" 10-year-old: "No, just her neck and collars." Mom: "GET THAT DOG INTO THE MUDROOM!" Send 10-year-old to scrub up like a surgeon and change clothes.

9:30: Pay bills and write a thank you note.

9:45: Shower for Mom . . . trying to wash away bad attitude and start the day over fresh. Take my cof fee into the shower with me (on my second cup by now).

10:00: Sit children down to eat warm granola.

10:05: Discover all the prep dishes still in the sink (9-year-old: "I rinsed them, though.").

10:15: Clean kitchen. Pour juice for girls.

10:20: Wipe up juice from the floor, spilled by 2-year-old.

10:30: Wrestle said 2-year-old into appropriate clothing.

10:45: Gather library books.

11:00: Think about doing hair, gather supplies.

11:15: Decide to write down this crazy day, quickly log the events thus far.

11:30: Think about my own hair and make up. Can do make-up in the car while waiting in the bank drive through; will do hair before departure.

PROJECTED:

11:30: Feed babies, do girls' hair while nursing.

11:45: Load up into car. Noon: Arrive at library . . . only 2 hours after expected ETA.

UPDATE:

11:30: Feed babies, working on hair.

11:45: Help 2-year-old dress.

11:47: Hear a gasp from 9-year-old—baby's diaper is leaking. Carrots. :(

11:50: Ask volunteer to change said diaper, begin doing my hair.

11:52: Hear another gasp, and a "Help!" from 10-year-old. Rush to the scene of diaper change on the floor.

11:53: Take over diaper change . . . which is a clothing change. Diaper was first affixed by another volunteer, and not put on properly. All mess was caught entirely by dress, rather than diaper. Change baby's clothes. She is very smiley and makes this process a cheerful one.

11:55: Ask 2-year-old to step away from contaminated area. Ask again. Shout "Get back!" as her footfall almost lands in said dress-diaper. She collapses in a weepy heap on the rug. Hug and console.

11:58: Wash hands. Continue to do my own hair.
Noon

12:05: Sound the All-Aboard to load up for the library . . .

12:17: Load up complete, driving out of driveway.
Realize I'm hungry. Forgot to eat breakfast, so I
eat a mini-clif bar and drink a glass of peach tea
snatched from the kitchen on the way out the door.
Find the Peach tea very soothing.

12:21: On the road.

12:27: Drive through bank window, fill out deposit slip.
Chat with teller over mini-computer screen.

12:34: Apply foundation, blush and mascara (while parked
in drive through).

12:37: Continue to drive towards library. Initiate car-
pick-up process, while moving. Entails picking
up everything within reach—without unbuckling.
Have packed laundry basket into the car
just for this.

12:47: Drive through post office mail box.

12:50: Drive through library drop off box to return books
(saves carrying that heavy basket twice!)

12:55: Check for messy faces and hair, fix as needed.

1:02: Out of car, walking to library.

1:20: Change messy diaper for baby in library restroom.

1:30: Begin chatting with sweet young Momma of three.
Continues until departure.

2:30: Begin book check-out at main desk. Chat with
clerk. Haven't seen her for a while, and I introduce
the twins. She gives me a hug! How lovely!

2:45: In car, beginning load up process. One of the big

sisters tosses 2-year-old, head first, over the back seat in a sack-of-potatoes fashion. Strong, stern verbal scolding brings big sister to tears.

3:15: Buy milk.

3:24: Pick up mail.

3:28: Unload process begun.

3:40: Begin making popcorn and tuna melts for lunch.

4:00: Sat at table to eat.

4:01: Change 2-year-old's messy diaper.

4:05: 2-year-old sad she can't sit on my lap to eat. In room.

4:11: Melt baby food after digging it out of the chest freezer and chopping it out of trays.

4:18: Feed babies.

4:25: Put babies in swings. Unhappy!

4:30: Sit to write update. Babies crying.

4:33: Comfort, soothe, move to crib.

4:39: Babies still crying.

4:40: Babies mostly asleep after pacifiers reinserted, blankies recuddled and retucked in.

4:42: All is quiet. Big girls in bed.

4:43: Pour glass of peach tea, sit to read and refuel before clean up.

4:45: Put baby food cubes into bags and replace in freezer. Pour tea. Eat a tuna melt.

4:50: Go to car to get forgotten cell phone.

4:53: Take photo of precious 2-year-old sleeping snuggled under covers. E-mail to Austin.

4:55: Sit to read a bit, eating popcorn.

5:11: Baby crying. Gave her a pacifier, and she returns to

Dreamland.

5:32: Sigh and stop reading. Commence lunch clean up and dinner preparation.

5:45: Call Mom and Dad to touch base and say hello. Wash dishes and fold laundry while chatting.

6:03: Answer call from Austin.

6:08: Get oldest three up to help with crazy-fast house pick up.

6:19: Austin and work "helper" home.

6:35: Nurse babies.

6:50: Cook dinner, thaw baby food cubes.

7:15: Serve dinner, feed babies.

7:35: Austin bathe babies.

8:00: Babies tucked in.

8:05: Kiddos preparing for bed—jammies, teeth brushing, etc.

8:35: Sit at computer to unwind a bit, write.

8:55: Begin dishes/kitchen clean up.

9:30: Call Mom to chat while washing dishes

10: 00: Chat with Austin.

11: 20: Clean bathroom.

MIDNIGHT

12: 05: Feed babies.

12: 15: Shower.

12: 45: My head hits the pillow.